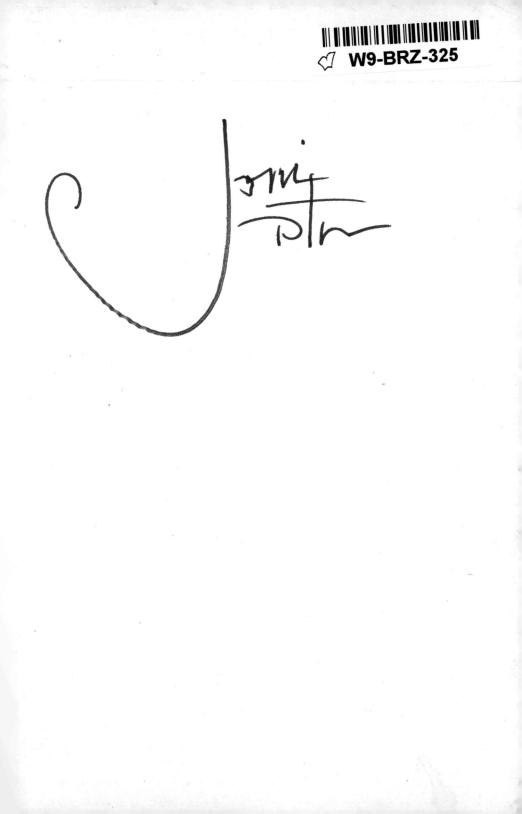

Joni

Joni

by Joni Eareckson
with Joe Musser

ZONDERVAN
PUBLISHING HOUSE OF THE ZONDERVAN CORPORATION
GRAND RAPIDS, MICHIGAN 49506

Names and identities of some of the persons and places in this book have been changed in order to protect their privacy or prevent embarrassment to them or their families.

JONI

© 1976 by Joni Eareckson and Joe Musser

Third printing   September 1976

Library of Congress Cataloging in Publication Data

Eareckson, Joni.
  Joni.

    1. Tetraplegia — Personal narratives.
2. Eareckson, Joni.   I.   Musser, Joe, joint
author.   II.   Title.
RC406.T4E18   362.4'3'0926[B]   76-10450

Printed in the United States of America

To the glory of the Lord Jesus Christ
. . . and lovingly dedicated to mom . . .
through whom He has especially expressed
His kindness and love. Through her
patient and understanding heart, I
have drawn much more than strength.

Preface

Isolated, by itself, what is a minute? Merely a measurement of time. There are 60 in an hour, 1,440 in a day. At seventeen, I had already ticked off more than 9,000,000 of them in my life.

Yet, in some cosmic plan, this single minute was isolated. Into these particular sixty seconds was compressed *more significance than all the millions of minutes marking my life prior to this instant.*

So many actions, sensations, thoughts, and feelings were crowded into that fragment of time. How can I describe them? How can I begin to catalog them?

I recall so clearly the details of those few dozen seconds — seconds destined to change my life forever. And there was no warning or premonition.

What happened on July 30, 1967, was the beginning of an incredible adventure which I feel compelled to share because of what I have learned.

Oscar Wilde wrote: "In this world there are only two tragedies. One is not getting what one wants, and the other is getting it." To rephrase his thought, I suggest there are likewise only two joys. One is having God answer all your prayers; the other is not receiving the answer to all your prayers. I believe this because I have found that God knows my needs infinitely better than I know them. And He is utterly dependable, no matter which direction our circumstances take us.

JONI EARECKSON

"We are handicapped on all sides, but we are never frustrated; we are puzzled, but never in despair. We are persecuted, but we never have to stand it alone: we may be knocked down but we are never knocked out! Every day we experience something of the death of Jesus, so that we may also know the power of the life of Jesus in these bodies of ours. . . . We wish you could see how all this is working out for your benefit, and how the more grace God gives, the more thanksgiving will redound to his glory. This is the reason we never collapse."

—2 Cor. 4:8-10, 15,16, Phillips

One

The hot July sun was setting low in the west and gave the waters of Chesapeake Bay a warm red glow. The water was murky, and as my body broke the surface in a dive, its cold cleanness doused my skin.

In a jumble of actions and feelings, many things happened simultaneously. I felt my head strike something hard and unyielding. At the same time, clumsily and crazily, my body sprawled out of control. I heard or felt a loud electric buzzing, an unexplainable inner sensation. It was something like an electrical shock, combined with a vibration—like a heavy metal spring being suddenly and sharply uncoiled, its "sprong" perhaps muffled by the water. Yet it wasn't really a sound or even a feeling — just a sensation. I felt no pain.

I heard the underwater sound of crunching, grinding sand. I was lying face down on the bottom. *Where? How did I get here? Why are my arms tied to my chest?* My thoughts screamed. *Hey! I'm caught!*

I felt a small tidal undercurrent lift me slightly and let me settle once more on the bottom. Out of the corner of my eye, I saw light above me. Some of the confusion left. I remembered diving into the bay. *Then what? Am I caught in a fishnet or something? I need to get out!* I tried to kick. *My feet must be tied or caught, too!*

Panic seized me. With all my will power and strength, I tried to break free. Nothing happened. Another tidal swell lifted and rolled.

What's wrong? I hit my head. Am I unconscious? Trying to move is like trying to move in a dream. Impossible. But I'll drown! Will I wake up in time? Will someone see me? I can't be unconscious, or I wouldn't be aware of what's happening. No, I'm alive.

I felt the pressure of holding my breath begin to build. I'd have to breathe soon.

Another tidal swell gently lifted me. Fragments of faces, thoughts, and memories spun crazily across my consciousness. My friends. My parents. Things I was ashamed of. Maybe God was calling me to come and explain these actions.

"Joni!" A somber voice echoed down some eerie corridor, almost as a summons. God? Death?

I'm going to die! I don't want to die! Help me, please.

"Joni!"

Doesn't anyone care that I'm here? I've got to breathe!

"Joni!" That voice! Muffled through the waters, it sounded far off. Now it was closer. "Joni, are you all right?"

Kathy! My sister sees me. Help me, Kathy! I'm stuck!

The next tidal swell was a little stronger than the rest and lifted me a bit higher. I fell back on the bottom, with broken shells, stones, and sand grating into my shoulders and face.

"Joni, are you looking for shells?"

No! I'm caught down here — grab me! I can't hold my breath any longer.

"Did you dive in here? It's so shallow," I heard Kathy clearly now.

Her shadow indicated she was now above me. I struggled inwardly against panic, but I knew I had no more air. Everything was going dark.

I felt Kathy's arms around my shoulders, lifting. *Oh, please, dear God. Don't let me die!*

Kathy struggled, stumbled, then lifted again. *Oh, God, how much longer?* Everything was black, and I felt I was falling while being lifted. Just before fainting, my head broke the water's surface. *Air!* Beautiful, life-giving, salt-tinged air. I choked in oxygen so quickly, I almost gagged. Gasping, I gulped in mouthfuls.

"Oh, thank You, God — thank You!" I managed.

"Hey, are you okay?" Kathy asked. I blinked to clear my mind and dissolve the confusion. It didn't seem to work because I saw my arm slung lifelessly over Kathy's shoulder, yet I felt it was still tied to my chest.

I looked down at my chest. My arms were not tied. I realized with a growing horror that my limbs were dangling motionlessly. I couldn't move them!

In the confusion, Kathy took charge. She called to a nearby swimmer on an inflated raft. Together they wrestled me onto it and pushed it toward shore. I heard the raft beneath me slide against the sandy beach.

I tried to get up but felt pinned against the raft. People began to hurry over to see what had happened. Soon there was a crowd hovering above me, faces looking down in curiosity. Their stares and whispers made me feel embarrassed, uncomfortable, and even more confused.

"Kathy, please make them leave."

"Yes, everyone stand back! Someone call an ambulance. Move away, please. She needs air," Kathy instructed.

Kathy's boyfriend, Butch, knelt beside me. His lean frame shielded me from the crowd, now moving back. "You okay, kid?" he asked. His large dark eyes, usually smiling and full of good-natured fun, were clouded with concern.

"Kathy — I can't move!" I was frightened. I could see they were, too.

Kathy nodded.

"Hold me!"

"I am, Joni." She lifted my hands to show that she was grasping them firmly.

"But I can't feel it. Squeeze me."

Kathy bent over and held me close. I couldn't feel her hug.

"Can you feel this?" She touched my leg.

"No," I said,

"This?" She squeezed my forearm,

"No!" I cried. "I can't feel it!"

"How about this?" Her hand slid from my arm to rest on my shoulder.

"Yes! Yes, I can feel that!"

Relief and joy suddenly came over us. At last, somewhere on my body, I could feel something. As I lay there on the sand, I began to piece things together. I had hit my head diving; I must have injured something to cause this numbness. I wondered how long it would last.

"Don't worry," I reassured Butch and Kathy — and myself. "The Lord won't let anything happen to me. I'll be all right."

I heard the wail of a siren. Soon the ambulance pulled up and doors opened. In less than a minute, attendants efficiently lifted me onto a stretcher. Somehow their starched white uniforms were comforting as they carefully placed me in the back of the ambulance. The crowd of curious onlookers followed.

Kathy started to climb up into the ambulance.

Butch took her hand and said softly, "I'll follow in the car." Then he nodded sternly to the driver. "Be careful with her," he instructed.

The siren began to wail, and we headed away from the beach.

I looked up at the attendant riding beside me and said, "I hate to put you to all this trouble. I think once I catch my breath I'll be okay. I'm sure the numbness will wear off shortly."

He didn't say anything but reached over and brushed sand off my face, smiled, and looked away. *I*

*wish he'd say something to let me know I'll be all right –
that I'll be going home as soon as the doctors at the
hospital check me over,* I thought.

But no comforting words were offered. I was left to
my own thoughts and prayers as the siren wailed. I
looked through the window at the city speeding by outside.

The Lord is my shepherd . . .

People on curbs stared curiously.

I shall not want . . .

Cars pulled over to let us pass.

He maketh me to lie down in green pastures . . .

The ambulance slowed and turned down a busy
boulevard.

He restoreth my soul . . .

I could not collect my thoughts enough to pray. I
clung to memorized promises from the Bible.

*Yea, though I walk through the valley of the shadow
of death, I will fear no evil: for thou art with me. . . .*

Suddenly the ambulance siren growled into silence.
The driver backed up to the doors of the hospital, and the
attendants quickly began to ease my stretcher out. As
they swung me smoothly through the doors, I saw the
sign:

EMERGENCY ENTRANCE

NO PARKING

Emergency Vehicles Only

By now the city sky was dark; the sun had set. I was
cold and longed to be home.

Inside, the emergency area was alive with activity. I
was taken into a room and placed on a hospital table with
wheels. The light hurt my eyes. As I turned my face to
avoid its glare, I could see all the equipment and
supplies arranged in ready rows. Bottles, gauze, bandages, trays, scissors, scalpels, jars, packets with long,
medical-sounding names, and unfamiliar shapes were all
about. The antiseptic smells and pungent odors made me
slightly queasy.

A nurse strapped me to the table and wheeled me into one of the many small cubicles. She pulled privacy curtains around me. Again I struggled desperately to move my arms and legs. They were still numb and motionless. *I feel so helpless. I'm getting sick. I'm scared.* Tears welled up in my eyes.

"Can't you tell me what's happened to me?" I begged.

The nurse merely shrugged and began to take off my rings. "The doctor will be here soon. Now, I'm going to put your jewelry in this envelope. Regulations."

"How long do I have to stay here? Can I go home tonight?"

"I'm sorry. You'll have to ask the doctor. Regulations." Her answer was emotionless and reminded me of a telephone recording.

Another nurse came into the cubicle with forms to fill out.

"Name, please."

"Joni Eareckson."

"Johnny? J-o-h-n-n-y?"

"No. It's pronounced Johnny — after my father — but it's spelled J-o-n-i. Last name is E-a-r-e-c-k-s-o-n." Then I gave her my address, my folks' name and number and asked her to call them.

"Do you have Blue Cross?"

"I don't know. Ask my folks — or my sister. She's probably outside. She was with me at the beach. Her name is Kathy. Ask her."

The nurse with the clipboard left. The other put the envelope with my belongings in it on a nearby table. Then she opened a drawer and pulled out a big pair of shears.

"W-what are you going to do?" I stammered.

"I've got to remove your swimming suit."

"But don't cut it! It's brand-new. I just got it — and it's my fav—"

"Sorry. Regulations," She repeated. The heavy *ch-cluk, ch-cluk, ch-cluk* of the shears echoed off the plaster walls. She pulled the ruined scraps of material off and dropped them in a waste can. She didn't even care. The suit didn't mean a thing to her. I wanted to cry.

She put a sheet over me and left. I felt embarrassed and uncomfortable. The sheet slipped down, exposing part of my breasts, and I couldn't move to pull it back up. Frustration and fear finally brought a flood of hot tears as I began to sense the seriousness of the situation.

Yea, though I walk through the valley of the shadow of death, I will fear no evil; for thou art with me. . . .

I fought back the tears and tried to think of other things. *I wonder if Kathy called mom and dad. I wonder if Dick knows yet.*

A man in dark tweed slacks and white lab coat pulled the curtains and stepped into the cubicle.

"I'm Dr. Sherrill," he said pleasantly while flipping through pages on a clipboard. "And your name is Joanie?"

"It's pronounced Johnny. I'm named after my father." *Must I go through this explanation with everyone?*

"Okay, Joni, let's see what's happened to you."

"Dr. Sherrill, when can I go home?"

"Tell me, do you feel this?" He had a long pin and was apparently pricking my feet and legs.

"N-no — I can't feel that."

"How about this?"

Gritting my teeth, I shut my eyes to concentrate, hoping to feel something — anything.

"Nothing."

He was holding my arm and pressing the pin against my limp fingers, wrist, and forearm. *Why can't I feel anything?* He touched the upper arm. Finally I felt a small sting in my shoulder.

"Yes, I feel that. I had feeling there at the beach."

Dr. Sherrill took out his pen and began to write on the clipboard.

Other medical staff people began to appear. Amidst the clatter and clutter of tubes, bottles, and trays, I heard Dr. Sherrill ask another doctor to come over. He went through the pin routine with the other doctor, and the two of them conferred in subdued voices near the head of my table. The language of medical terms and jargon was unfamiliar to me.

"Looks like a fracture-dislocation."

"Uh-huh. I'd say at the fourth and fifth cervical level judging from her areas of feeling."

"We'll need to get to it. X-rays won't tell if there's continuity or not."

"Shall I order O-R prepped?"

"Yes. Stat. And try again to reach her parents."

Dr. Sherrill's associate left quickly, followed by one of the nurses. Dr. Sherrill whispered instructions to the brusque nurse who had destroyed my swimsuit, and she left, too.

I watched someone wipe my arm with a cotton ball and stick a needle into the vein. I felt nothing.

Out of the corner of my eye, I saw Dr. Sherrill holding a pair of electric hair clippers. There was a loud click and buzzing sound as they were turned on. *What on earth are those for?* I wondered. With growing terror, I realized they were moving toward my head.

"No," I cried. "Please! Not my hair! Please," I sobbed. I felt the clippers sliding across my scalp and saw chunks of damp blond hair fall beside my head and onto the floor. An attendant was preparing a soapy lather. She picked up a razor and walked toward me. *She's going to shave my head! Oh, dear God, no! Don't let them!*

The room began to spin. My stomach churned, and I felt faint.

Then I heard a high-pitched noise, something between a buzz and a squeal. *It's a drill!* Someone held my head, and the drill began grinding into the side of my skull.

I began to feel drowsy — *probably the shot they gave me*. I was falling asleep. More panic. *What if I don't wake up? Won't I ever see Dick again? Kathy? Mom and dad? Oh, God, I'm afraid!*

I saw faces. I heard voices. But nothing made sense. The room began to grow dark and the noise faded.

For the first time since the dive I felt relaxed, even

peaceful. It no longer mattered that I was paralyzed, lying naked on a table with a shaved head. The drill no longer seemed threatening either. I drifted into a deep sleep.

*   *   *   *

Coming out of the blackness, I thought I heard the drill and tried to wake up enough to shout at them to stop. I didn't want them drilling when I was awake. But no words came. I tried to open my eyes. The room was spinning.

The noise in the background became more distinct, too. It wasn't the drill; it was only an air conditioner.

My head and vision began to clear, and for a moment I couldn't remember where I was or why I was afraid of a drill. Then memory returned.

I looked up at a ventilator grill above my head, at the high, ancient, cracked plaster ceiling. I tried to turn my head to see the rest of my surroundings, but I couldn't move at all. Sharp pains on each side of my head resisted my attempt to move. I sensed that the holes they had drilled in my skull had something to do with this. Out of the corner of my eyes, I could see large metal tongs attached to a spring-cable device pulling my head away from the rest of my body. It took an unusual amount of strength — both mental and physical — just to learn this much about my new surroundings.

During those first days I drifted in and out of consciousness. The drugs sent me off into a dream world, a nightmare devoid of reality. Hallucinations were common and often frightening. Dreams, impressions, and memories blurred together in confusion so that I often thought I was losing my mind.

A recurring nightmare came to me out of the surrealistic world induced by the drugs. In this dream, I was with Jason Leverton, my steady all through high school. We were in some unusual setting waiting to be judged. I was naked and tried to cover myself in shame. In the nightmare, I was on my feet, standing before a figure dressed in robes. I knew him as an "apostle." He didn't say anything, but I knew somehow that I was being judged. Suddenly he pulled out a long sword and swung it in my direction, striking me square on the neck and cutting off my head. Then I'd wake up crying and afraid. This same dream haunted me again and again.

Other hallucinagenic experiences from the drugs turned even the crazy world of dreams inside out. Vivid colors, shapes, and figures swelled and contracted into strange and unusual patterns. I saw "frightening" colors, "peaceful" patterns — shapes and colors that represented feelings, moods and emotions.

Someone's loud moaning woke me from my nightmare. I didn't know how much time had elapsed since my last period of consciousness, but this time I was face down! How had I gotten in that position? The tongs were still in place. Their pressure against the sides of my head caused more mental and psychological pain than physical discomfort.

I discovered I was encased in some kind of a canvas frame. There was an opening for my face, and I could see only an area immediately beneath my bed. A pair of legs with white shoes and nylon hose stood within this narrow field of vision.

"Nurse," I called out weakly.

"Yes. I'm here."

"W-hat — where — uh — " I stammered, trying to phrase my question.

"Sh-h-h. Don't try to talk. You'll tire yourself," she said. From her pleasant voice and reassuring manner, I knew she wasn't the nurse who had cut off my bathing suit or the one who had shaved my head. I felt her hand on the back of my shoulder.

"Just try and rest. Go back to sleep if you can. You're in ICU. You've had surgery, and we'll take good care of you. So, don't worry. Okay?" She patted my shoulder. It was such a pleasant sensation to have feeling somewhere — except in my head, where the tongs bit into the flesh and bone.

Gradually I became aware of my surroundings. I

learned that the device I called a bed was really a Stryker
Frame. It looked like I was in a canvas sandwich held
tightly by straps. Two nurses or orderlies would come
every two hours to turn me over. They'd place a canvas
frame on top of me, and while a nurse held the weights
attached to the "ice tong" calipers (and my head), they
would deftly flip me 180 degrees. Then they would remove the frame I had been lying on and make sure I was
ready for my two-hour shift in this new position. I had two
views — the floor and the ceiling.

Eventually I learned that my Stryker Frame was in
an eight-bed ICU ward and that ICU was short for *inten-
sive care unit*. I'd never heard the phrase used before but
figured out it must be for serious cases. Patients were
only allowed visitors for five minutes per hour — and
then just by family members.

As the hours blurred into days, I got to know my
roommates better. Through snatches of conversation,
instructions of doctors, and other sounds, I pieced together quite a bit.

The man in a bed next to mine groaned constantly.
On the change of nurses for the morning shift, I heard a
night nurse explain to her replacement in a whisper, "He
shot his wife and then tried to kill himself. He probably
won't make it. He's to be restrained."

That explained the sound of chains rattling — he
had been handcuffed to his bed!

A woman in one of the other beds moaned through
the night. She was begging the nurses to give her a
cigarette or ice cream.

Judy was a young girl like myself. But she was in a
coma as the result of injuries sustained in a car accident.

Tom was a young man who was there because of a
diving accident. It's funny. I knew Tom had broken his
neck but didn't understand that *I* had. No one told me.

Tom could not even breathe on his own. I learned
this when I asked a nurse what a certain sound was. She
explained it was Tom's resuscitation equipment.

When we learned of the similarity of our accidents,
we began to send notes back and forth. "Hi, I'm Tom,"

his first note said by way of introduction. Nurses and visitors wrote our notes and were our couriers.

At night, when the flurry of activity was less intense, I'd hear the moaning and groaning of others in my ICU ward. Then I'd listen for the reassuring sound of Tom's resuscitation equipment. Since I couldn't turn to see him, the sound was comforting. I felt a kinship with him and wondered what he looked like. *Tomorrow*, I thought, *I'll ask for his photo.*

Later that night, the resuscitator stopped. The silence was as loud as an explosion. Panic seized me, and my voice choked as I tried to call out for help. I heard nurses as they rushed to Tom's bedside.

"His resuscitator is down! Get a new one, stat!" someone ordered.

I could hear footsteps running down the tile hallway and the metallic sounds of the oxygen unit being removed. Another person was on the telephone at the nurses' station calling for emergency help. Within minutes, the room, hallway, and nurses' station were busy with urgent, whispered instructions and the confused commotion of crisis.

"Tom! Can you hear me, Tom?" a doctor called. Then snapped, "Where's that other resuscitator?"

"Shall we try artificial respiration, doctor?" asked a woman's voice.

My mind was spinning with the frustrations of my paralysis. I was helpless — and even if I could move, there was nothing I could do. Wide-eyed, I lay there staring past the ceiling into darkness.

"The orderly had to go downstairs for another unit. He's on his way."

"Keep up the mouth-to-mouth. We've got to keep him alive until — " the man's voice broke off.

I heard the doors of the elevator down the hall open and close and urgent running footsteps along with the rattle of equipment. The sounds were aimed toward the ICU ward and, with a sense of relief, I heard someone say, "I've got a unit. You want to make room?"

Then, with horror, I heard the chilling reply.

"Never mind. We've lost him. He's dead."

I felt the flesh on the back of my neck crawl. With mounting terror, I realized they were not talking about some unknown patient, some impersonal statistic. They were talking about Tom. *Tom was dead!*

I wanted to scream but was unable to. I was afraid of falling asleep that night, afraid that I, too, would not wake up.

The next day, my terror was no less intense. I grieved for a man I knew only through notes, and I began to think about my own situation. I was not dependent on a machine in order to breathe. But I was dependent on the IV — intravenous solutions — that put sustenance into my body and the catheter in my bladder that drained body wastes and poisons.

What if one of these fails? What if the tongs come loose from my head? What if — my brain was a frightened jumble.

A day or two later, a man was brought in with a similar injury. They put him on a Stryker Frame and put an oxygen tent around him.

Out of the corner of my eye, I could see what the frame was like. I could not see my own, but could now understand what happened each time they flipped me — two hours up, two hours down. Looking at him, I had the feeling that we were like steers being turned regularly on some huge barbecue spit. I was terrified each time they came to flip me.

The new patient was just as apprehensive. As the orderlies prepared to flip him one day, he cried out, "No, please don't flip me. I couldn't breathe when I was turned before! Don't flip me!"

"That's all right, mister. You'll be okay. We have to turn you. Doctor's orders. Ready, Mike? On three. One. Two. Three!"

"No! Please! I can't breathe! I'll pass out — I know it!"

"You'll be fine. Just relax."

They fixed the plastic tent for his oxygen and left. I could hear the man's labored, gasping breathing and prayed the two hours would pass quickly — for his sake as well as my own peace of mind.

Then, suddenly, the breathing stopped. Again there was commotion and activity as nurses and orderlies responded to the crisis. It was too late. Again.

Hot tears flowed from my eyes. Frustration and fear, my twin companions during those early hospital days, overtook me again. With a growing sense of horror and shock, I learned that the ICU ward was a room for the *dying*. I felt my own life was a fragile thing — not something I could take for granted.

Shortly thereafter, during one of the flipping sessions, I fainted and stopped breathing. But within minutes they had revived me, and I felt reassured by their efficiency and deep concern.

"We're going to take good care of you, Joni," comforted one doctor. After that, while every turn was still a frightening experience for me, I was conscious of the fact that the nurses and orderlies were more careful than before. Or so it seemed.

I began to notice how cold the ICU ward was. Nearly every patient was unconscious most of the time, so they were probably unaware of the coldness, but it began to bother me. I was afraid of catching cold. One of the orderlies had let it slip one day that a cold could be dangerous for me. Also dangerous was blood poisoning, which was somehow frequent in such cases. There was so much to be frightened about. Nothing seemed positive or hopeful.

Everyday doctors came to see me. Sometimes they came in pairs and discussed my case.

"She has total quadriplegia," one doctor explained to an associate, "the result of a diagonal fracture between the fourth and fifth cervical levels."

I knew I was paralyzed but didn't know why. Or for how long. No one ever explained anything to me about my injury.

Nurses said, "Ask the doctors."

Doctors said, "Oh, you're doing fine — just fine."

I suspected the worst — that I had a broken neck.

That thought alone frightened me. A vivid childhood memory came to me. It was the only "real" instance I knew of anyone breaking his neck. A man in the story *Black Beauty* fell from a horse and broke his neck. He *died*.

So, inwardly, I didn't want to hear about my accident, and mentally I began to tune out the medical staff's discussions.

I knew that I was in a room of dying people because *I was going to die*, just like Tom and the other man. They both had had injuries like mine. *I'm going to die, too*, I thought. *They're just afraid to tell me!*

Two

The days passed, marked only by recurring nightmares and the strain and discomfort of my canvas prison and metal tongs. I had finally decided that I probably wasn't going to die. While others in the ICU ward either died or got better and were transferred to regular hospital rooms, I stayed. I got no better, but no worse.

To take my mind off the anguish of the nightmares, from which I woke terrified and drenched with perspiration, I began to daydream, recalling all the events in my life before the accident.

I had had a happy life with my family and friends. We had never known tragedy firsthand. As far back as I could remember, there had been nothing but happiness surrounding our lives and home.

Daddy was probably the reason — the man I was named for, Johnny Eareckson. Born in 1900, dad took the best of both the nineteenth and twentieth centuries. He is an incurable romantic and creative artist but is also in tune with technology. His father had a coal (fuel) business, and during his childhood, dad cared for the horses before and after school. He drew much knowledge from what he calls the "school of hard knocks," too. He had been attracted to unusual and difficult work because of what he felt it could teach him. His values are personal character, individual happiness, and spiritual development. If a man has these and can pass these qualities on to his children, only then does dad consider him successful.

Dad had done almost everything — from being a sailor to owning and managing his own rodeo! His life was filled with hobbies — horses, sculpture, painting, and building things — his handiwork literally covering the walls and shelves of our home.

I asked dad once, "How do you find time, with your work, to do all the things you do?"

He looked at me, his clear blue eyes sparkling, and replied, "Honey, it began during the Depression. Nobody had work. Most people sat around and felt sorry about themselves and complained. Me? Why, I could use my hands. Carving didn't cost anything. So, I built things from stuff others threw away. I kept busy with my hands all through the Depression. Guess the habit stuck."

It was also during those lean years that dad was an Olympic wrestler. He was National AAU Wrestling Champion, a five-time winner of national YMCA championship wrestling honors, and earned a berth on the U.S. Olympic team of 1932. During his days as a wrestler, he received an injury which makes him walk with a slight limp today.

As a young man, he was active in church youth work. In his twenties and early thirties, dad was "Cap'n John" to the church young people. He took the kids camping, on overnight trips, hiking, and on retreats. He had an old flat-bed truck and would pile kids, sleeping bags, cookstove, and supplies on board and leave for one of "Cap'n John's Tours." They were memorable times and often made an impression on many of the young people. One young woman was especially impressed by "Cap'n John." She was the energetic and vivacious Margaret "Lindy" Landwehr who took a natural interest in

athletics and the outdoors and thus gained the attention
of "Cap'n John."

Soon "Lindy" fell in love with "Cap'n John" and he
with her. Many of their dates were crowded, however, for
"Cap'n John" brought the entire youth group along!

As an expression of his love, dad worked night and
day and built a house for mom as a wedding present. It
was toward the end of the Depression and money was still
scarce, so he scoured the area with his truck. From an old
sailing ship, he salvaged huge beams for the foundation
and rafters.

While driving one day, he saw some men demolish-
ing a rock wall.

"What are you going to do with those rocks?" he
asked.

"Why?"

"I'll be glad to haul them away," dad replied.

"Okay," the foreman grunted, "just make sure
they're gone by Friday. We've got a job to do here."

"Yessir!" shouted dad. He began the remarkable
job of single-handedly moving boulders — most weighing more than a hundred pounds. He did it by himself,
somehow maneuvering them onto his truck. After many
trips, he had enough for his house. Today two beautiful,
huge stone fireplaces are the result of that labor.

The same kind of thing happened when he needed
lumber, bricks, and other building supplies. Finally his
dream house was completed. He and his bride moved in
and have lived there since.

Daddy had the same active interest in business and
civic affairs. Years ago, he started his own flooring business.

He said, "I guess I'm too independent to work for
somebody else. I love my family too much to be tied down
to someone else's schedule and interests. By being my
own boss, if I want to take off a day and drive my family to
the ocean or take 'em horseback riding, I don't have to
ask anyone. I just put a sign on the door, lock up, and
go."

And we did. We took many trips and vacations, and

they were so much fun that it's difficult to believe they were also part of our education. Dad taught us geography and geology during "survival" backpack outings in the desert or mountains. He showed us how to distinguish between the tracks of various animals, their calls, their ways — things we could never learn in the city.

He introduced us to horseback riding almost as soon as we could sit up. I was in the saddle at age two. In fact, daddy often bragged, "Do you remember the time our whole family rode a hundred miles on horseback? It was from Laramie to Cheyenne, Wyoming. Remember, Joni? You were only four years old! Youngest ever to ride in the Cheyenne Ride." When we were a bit older, he took us pack-riding in the wilderness of the Medicine Bow range where we acquired a deep appreciation for God and His creation.

Dad taught us all to ride gracefully balanced and gave us lessons in show horsemanship. "Just ride in a rolling motion with the horse," he'd say, "not like the beginners — bouncing on the horse. It's almost impossible to synchronize your up and down bounces to the horse's movements. You've got to roll with him, not bounce."

Dad was always even-tempered and amiable. Nothing or no one ever ruffled him. Not once during all our growing-up years did I see him lose his temper. Our behavior then was based on "not hurting daddy." We didn't do certain things because of "what it would do to daddy," not because it was simply questionable or wrong.

When dad came to the hospital for the brief visits allowed in the ICU ward, he tried to communicate the same genial, positive spirit I'd always known. But no matter how much he tried to appear relaxed and hopeful, his clouded blue eyes, usually so clear and sparkling, betrayed his nervousness. His weathered, gnarled hands shook as they revealed his true feelings. He was afraid and hurt. The daughter he loved and named after himself was lying helpless in a sandwich of canvas and a tangle of IV and catheter tubes.

The hospital was no place for this man who had spent a lifetime outdoors as an active athlete. His pain and restlessness were difficult to hide.

It hurt me to see what my accident had done to him. *"Why, God?"* I asked. *"Why are You doing this?"*

There was an unusually strong bond of love which tied us together as a family. Mom was a source of that strength. She, too, loved the outdoors and athletic competition and shared dad's interests. In fact, it was she who taught us girls to play tennis. Swimming and hiking were also things we did as a family.

Mom, with her strong character and loving personality, worked as hard as daddy to see that we had a happy home. There was seldom any disagreement between my parents, and their obvious love for one another was reflected in our lives and made us feel wanted and secure.

After the accident, mom was the one who took charge at the hospital. She stayed there around the clock the first four days, catching short naps on a sofa in the lounge. She did not leave until she was absolutely certain I was out of danger.

Since we were such a close family, my sisters shared my parents' concern. Kathy, twenty, dark-haired, pretty, and shy, was the one who had pulled me from the water and saved my life.

Jay, twenty-three at the time of my accident, was the sister I was closest to. She was quiet and graceful, her long, blond hair lightened by constant exposure to sun and swimming.

Jay was married and the mother of a little girl named Kay. In spite of her family responsibilities, she found time to come to the hospital and be with me, and I looked forward to her visits. If my Stryker Frame had me facing down, she'd lie down on the floor. There she'd spread out *Seventeen* magazines for us to read together. And she tried to brighten my corner of the room with plants and posters, although "regulations" soon required that they be removed.

Linda, my oldest sister, was married and had three

small children. Because she was about ten years older than I was, I was not as close to her as to Kathy and Jay.

The memories of our good times as a family did help to take my mind off the pain and nightmares. I also recalled the good experiences of my high school years and the friends I had made then.

Woodlawn Senior High School was located in a scenic part of our suburban Baltimore area. The two-story brick complex was situated in the midst of a campus that made full use of the outdoors. Sidewalks were lined with trees, and a small stream wound through the grassy grounds. Art students were often scattered around the picturesque, landscaped campus, sketching or painting.

Out back, on the athletic field, were ball diamonds, track courses, tennis courts, and lacrosse courts. Lacrosse was the sport I loved most. In fact, being named captain of our girls' lacrosse team in my senior year meant more to me than my nomination to the Honor Society.

As a sophomore at Woodlawn, I had come into contact with an organization called *Young Life*, a religious-oriented youth work that ministers primarily to high school kids. I had noticed that lots of the "neat" kids, the achievers, the popular ones, were Christian kids from *Young Life*, so when I heard about a "fantastic retreat" *Young Life* was sponsoring, I wanted to go.

"Mom," I begged, "you've simply got to let me go. Please?" I was fifteen, a young girl searching for identity and meaning to life.

The *Young Life* weekend was held in Natural Bridge, Virginia. Crowds of kids from Baltimore area high schools converged on this tiny community for a weekend crammed with fun and challenges to consider what the Bible had to say about our relationship to God.

Carl Nelson, the *Young Life* camp speaker, shared how the gospel begins with God's glory and His righteousness. "That standard of righteousness was expressed through the Ten Commandments," he told us.

Carl opened his Bible and read "and by the law comes knowledge of sin."

"And so, gang," he went on, "it's impossible to reach heaven by trying to stick to a list of moral do's and don'ts. There's just no way any one of us can live up to those commandments God has laid down."

The meeting broke up, and I wandered out into the fall night air. *Me, a sinner?* I'd never really understood what that word meant. However, now I saw my rebellion in the light of God's perfection. I knew *I* was a lost *sinner*, no matter how strange it sounded.

Well, I obviously can't save myself, so who. . . .

Then everything that Carl had shared thus far that weekend began to make sense. *That's why Jesus, God's Son, had come!*

"He being God in the flesh fulfilled the law and lived the perfect life. And when He died, He was paying the penalty of your sin." I recalled Carl's words.

I sat down and leaned back against a tree and looked up at the silent expanse of stars, half-expecting to see something — I don't know what. Only flickering specks blinked back. Yet, as I looked, I was overwhelmed by the love of God. I closed my eyes. "Oh, God, I see my sin; yet I also see Your mercy. Thank You for sending Your Son, Jesus, to die for me. I've decided in my heart not to do those things which will grieve You anymore. Instead of doing things my way, I want Christ to sit on the throne of my life and lead me. Thank You for saving me from sin and giving me eternal life." I got up and ran back to the room, anxious to tell my friend Jackie how God had saved me.

I had always heard how much God loved me as I was growing up. Mom and dad were Christians and members of the Bishop Cummings Reformed Episcopal Church in Catonsville.

But in my early teens I was looking for my own way and life style, and I didn't have time for God. I had experimented with many things to find out where I fit into life. At first I thought popularity and dates were the answer. Then I thought the discipline of athletics was where I would find it. But now my searching ended. All the pieces of the puzzle fit together, and it all made sense!

*Jesus, God's Son, had come to save me and make me a
whole person.*

A great flood of personal joy came to me that night,
and I made a decision to invite Jesus Christ into my heart
and life. I didn't fully understand it all, but I was to learn
that God is patient, loving, forgiving, and tolerant of our
mistakes.

I heard two concepts presented that weekend which
I had never clearly understood before. I learned that I
was a sinner because I wasn't able, nor was anyone able,
to live up to God's standards for behavior. That's why He
allowed His Son, the Lord Jesus Christ, to die for *me*. It
was an emotional, meaningful moment when I realized
Jesus died for me, personally.

Then I heard about an exciting concept called
"the abundant life." Our counselor explained that Jesus
came to die for our sins, but that He also came to give
us "abundant life" (John 10:10). In my immature mind,
the abundant life meant I'd lose weight or have new
popularity and dates at school, lots of friends, and good
grades.

My concept of what was meant by the abundant life
was completely wrong, of course, and by the time I was a
junior in high school, things had slipped for me. I had
expected, as a new Christian, to find security and purpose in *things* — the things I'd based my spiritual life on
— going to church, singing in choir, serving as a *Young
Life* club officer. My whole focus was on these things, not
on God. My life revolved around temporal values, my
own ego and desires.

About this time, I met Jason Leverton. Jason was a
handsome, muscular, and personable guy. With his
broad shoulders, serious brown eyes, and thick light-
colored hair, he was called the "Blond Flash" by his
wrestling teammates for his speed and ability in state
champion competition. Jason and I dated regularly and
were always together at school and social functions.

Dad was especially fond of Jason because of his own
keen interest in wrestling. It was not surprising for me to
play second fiddle to dad when Jason came to visit.

Frequently they would good-naturedly "take on" one another, demonstrating unusual wrestling holds or pins.

Jason was lots of fun. He and I shared secrets and our plans for the future. We planned to go to college together, probably even get married one day.

We had a favorite place — a nearby park — where we'd take walks and talk. Jason was also active in *Young Life* so these times were often used for sharing spiritual thoughts and praying together. Sometimes I'd even climb down the drain pipe outside my bedroom window and meet him after curfew — until mom caught me one night! She made certain I obeyed curfew rules after that.

It was about the time Jason and I started to get romantically serious that real conflicts started. We both were seniors in high school and knew there were stated limits in expressing our affection for one another. But neither of us had the inner resources capable of dealing with problems of temptation.

We would often go driving or horseback riding. Many times we'd ride out to an open meadow surrounded by beautiful woods, deep blue skies, and magnificent summer clouds. The sights, sounds, and smells of the country were terribly romantic and erotic. Before we realized what was happening, innocent, youthful expressions of love for one another — hand-holding, hugging, kissing — gave way to caressing, touching, and passions neither of us could control. We wanted to stop, but often when we found ourselves in a secluded spot, we fell into each other's arms. Our mutual lack of self-restraint bothered us tremendously.

"Jason — why can't we stop? What's wrong with us?" I asked one night.

"I don't know. I know we shouldn't mess around, but — "

"Jason, we've got to stop seeing each other for awhile. It's the only way. I can't stop. You can't either. Every time we get alone, we — uh — we sin. If we're really serious about repenting of all this, then we're just going to have to stay away from each other for awhile so we can avoid temptation."

Jason was silent awhile. Then he agreed. "Maybe we should."

He suggested that I might enjoy dating his friend Dick Filbert, a sensitive, mature Christian. I guess he thought if I was dating someone else, it might as well be a friend. That way we'd still have an indirect contact.

Dick was tall, lean, and good-looking — like Jason — but there the similarity ended. Dick was quiet, shy, but more expressive. An aura of casualness surrounded him right down to his worn jeans and moccasins, and his soft voice reflected a peace and serenity. Dick's eyes, bright and blue, could quiet any storm in my soul, and his presence was a strong, unmoving rock that I could cling to in times of confusion.

During my senior year, my time was divided between Jason and Dick. I tried to avoid romantic interest in either of them and to treat each as just a good friend. I relaxed by horseback riding, playing records and guitar, and I tried to learn more about the Christian life through *Young Life* Bible studies. Even my prayer times began to reflect more serious goals.

I was accepted for the fall term at Western Maryland College on academic recommendations. My life seemed to be falling in place, going somewhere — and yet it wasn't.

I remember lying in bed one morning shortly after graduation and thinking about all these things.

The summer sunlight flooded into my window. Filtered through leaves in the trees outside, it splattered into flickering points of dancing light across my bed and along the pink, rose-print wallpaper. I yawned and rolled over to look outside. When daddy built his dream house, he included these unique touches like the small "porthole" window near the floor beside my bed. I'd just turn over in bed and look down outside.

It was still early but I got up quickly and fished out a pair of Levi's and a pullover shirt from my dresser. As I dressed, my eyes turned once more to the black leather diploma folder on the dressing table. I ran my fingers over its grain and the embossed Old English lettering of my name and school crest. Just a few days earlier, I had walked down the aisle in cap and gown to receive that diploma.

"Breakfast!" Mom's voice downstairs punctuated my reverie.

"Coming, mom," I called. Bounding down the stairs, I pulled a chair up to the table.

"Are you going out to the ranch after church, Joni?" asked mom.

"Uh-huh. I know Tumbleweed's going to be ready for the summer horse show circuit but I want to spend more time with her, anyway."

The "ranch" was our family farm some twenty miles west of town. It was situated on a panoramic ridge in the rolling, picturesque river valley and was surrounded by state park land.

By the time I got there, the sun had already climbed high in the sky and the fragrance of new-mown hay was blown toward me. The breeze also caressed the tall wildflowers and grasses of the sloping meadows and gently tossed the uppermost branches in the sweet-smelling apple trees nearby. Humming softly and happily, I saddled Tumbleweed and swung up to mount her.

It was refreshing to be so far away from the dirt, noise and noxious smells of the city. In summer, Baltimore suffers from the industrial air pollution and sweltering humidity that rolls in from Chesapeake Bay. Here, in our own little paradise, we're free to enjoy the summer sun and air.

I pressed my thighs against Tumbleweed's sides and nudged her with my heels. The chestnut mare headed up the dusty dirt road at a walk. When we came to the pasture, I dug my heels again. Tumbleweed really didn't need the silent command. She knew there was room to run here without concern for potholes or rocks. Scattered across the field were several log-rail fence jumps. We cantered toward this first jump, a broad, four-foot solid rail fence. As I tightened my knees against Tumbleweed, I felt the smooth, precision strides of the big horse.

The experienced rider instinctively knows the right "feel" of a horse preparing to jump. Tumbleweed was experienced and so was I. We had won all kinds of ribbons and horse show awards. I knew the sound of hoofs — the proper cadence, pounding across the earthen course.

Smoothly, the horse lifted up and over the fence. Suspended for an instant, it was like flying. Nearly ten feet off the ground aboard Tumbleweed, I was exhilarated each time the mare jumped. After several runs, Tumbleweed was wet with sweaty lather.

I reined her to a slow trot and turned back toward the barn.

"Joni!"

Looking up, I saw dad astride his gray gelding galloping across the field toward me. Smiling, dad pulled his horse up.

"I saw her jump, Joni. She's in excellent shape. I think you'll both run away with the ribbons at next week's show!"

"Well, if we do, it'll be because you taught me everything I know about riding," I reminded dad.

By the time dad and I returned to the barn, unsaddled the horses and slapped them toward the corral, it was 4:30. "We'd better head for home. We don't want to be late for dinner," I said.

I recalled the pleasure of the previous perfect day, riding on my horse Tumbleweed under a beautiful summer sky. But inwardly I knew it was an elaborate form of escape. I didn't want to face the real issues. I wondered — *Lord, what am I going to do? I'm happy and content, grateful for the good things You supply – but deep down, I know something is wrong. I think I'm at the place where I need You to really work in my life.*

As I traced my spiritual progress over the last couple years, I realized I had not come far. Jason and I had broken up, true; and Dick was better for me in that regard. But I was still enslaved. Instead of "sins of the flesh," I was trapped by my "sins of the emotions" — anger, jealousy, resentment, and possessiveness. I had drifted through my last years of school. My grades dropped and, as a result, I began to fight with my parents. I lacked goals or the motivation to do well. It was obvious to me that I had not made much spiritual progress in the two years I'd been a Christian. It seemed no matter how hard I tried to improve, I was always a slave of my desires.

Now I was insistent with God. "Lord, if You're really there, do something in my life that will change me and turn me around. You know how weak I was with Jason. You know how possessive and jealous I am with Dick. I'm sick of the hypocrisy! I want You to work in my life for real. I don't know how — I don't even know, at this point, if You can. But I'm begging You — please do something in my life to turn it around!"

I had prayed that prayer just a short time before my accident. Now, lying encased in my Stryker Frame, I wondered if somehow God was answering my prayer.

Three

"The Bible says, 'Everything works together for good,' even your accident, Joni." Dick was trying to comfort me, but I wasn't listening too intently.

"I've already been in this stupid hospital a month," I complained, "and I haven't seen very much good!

"I can't sleep at night because of nightmares and hallucinations caused by the drugs. I can't move — I'm stuck in this dumb Stryker Frame! What's good? Tell me, Dickie, what's good about that?"

"I — I don't know, Joni. But I think we should claim God's promise. Let's trust Him that it will work out for good," Dick said quietly, patiently. "Want me to read something else?"

"No. I'm sorry. I didn't mean to jump on you like that. I guess I'm not really trusting the Lord, am I?"

"It's all right — " Dick was on the floor beneath my Stryker Frame looking up into my eyes. Incredible sadness and pity made his expressive eyes well with tears. He blinked and looked away. "Well," he said finally, "I gotta go now. See ya later, okay?"

Dick's faithfulness in visiting was one thing I clung
to during those first grim weeks, along with mom, dad,
Jackie, and Jay. Others, like Jason, came when they
could, too. The hospital personnel joked about all my
"cousins," and the "five minutes per hour for family
members" regulation was bent many times.

When mom and dad came, I always asked to be
flipped if I was facing the floor. While they joked and got
down on the floor if I was face down, I was deeply hurt
that they had to go through the indignity of crawling
around on the floor in order to visit with me.

I tried hard to kindle their hope and faith, too. As I
thought about my problems, it was easy to find others
around me in the hospital who were worse off than I. With
that in mind, I tried to cheer my folks and others who
came to visit. I even began to be pleasant to the hospital
staff.

It wasn't that my personality had become sweeter.
Rather, I was afraid people would stop coming to see me
if I got bitter and complained, so I worked at cheerfulness.

"My, you're in a good mood today," observed Anita,
one of the nurses from the day shift.

"Sure, why not? It's a gorgeous day."

"It's raining!"

"Not on me. I'm snug as a bug," I teased.

"Want me to come by later?"

"Would you? Yes — I'd like that, Anita." Although
she was assigned to duty elsewhere in the hospital, Anita
took a special interest in me. She often spent her lunch
hour with me, reading Robert Frost's poetry or just chatting. Since I'd already spent so much time in the inten-
sive care ward, many of the nurses were becoming my
friends. By now I was more accustomed to the routine and
regulations. And just as they sometimes bent some of the
rules when visitors came, so I began to overlook the
hospital's shortcomings as well.

Anita patted my shoulder and waved. "I'll see you
later, Joni." I heard her light footsteps click away down
the tiled hallway.

When she left, Jason came to visit. "Hi, kid," he grinned, "you look terrible. When do you get to leave here?"

"Not for awhile, I guess. I think I'm supposed to be learning something through all this," I answered. "Dickie says God is working in my life."

"God doesn't have anything to do with it! You got a busted neck, that's all. You can't lay back and say 'it's God's will' and let it go at that! You gotta fight it, Joni. And get better," Jason said sharply.

He looked at me, not knowing what else to say. Our relationship had been sort of "tabled" when we agreed to a cooling-off period. Now he was suggesting — if not by words, by the expression in his eyes and squeeze of his hand on my shoulder — that he still cared deeply.

"We gotta fight this thing, Joni. You gotta get better, y'hear?" His voice broke and he began to cry. "Forget the business about it being God's will that you're hurt. Fight it! Y'hear?"

He swore softly for added emphasis and said, "It doesn't make any sense. How could God — if there is a God — let it happen?"

"I know it seems that way, Jason. But Dickie says God must have some kind of reason for it."

"I dunno. Maybe I'm just bitter — cynical. But I don't feel God is interested any more. I don't think He's there."

This admission by Jason was the first step in his drifting away from trust in a loving God — his resignation that what happened was the result of blind, random forces.

I stared at the ceiling after he left. It had been a month, and I was still here. *What's wrong with me?* I wondered.

"Hello, lassie. How's m' favorite lass today?" I couldn't see him yet, but the voice was that of Dr. Harris. As his tall, redheaded frame came into my field of vision, I smiled and greeted him. Dr. Harris had been in the shock trauma unit of the hospital the night of my accident. He had taken a personal interest in me and followed my case. I was charmed by his Scottish brogue and the fact that he always referred to me as "lassie."

He picked up my charts and looked them over. "Hm-m. You're lookin' good, lassie. Feeling better?"

"I — I don't know. What's wrong with me, Dr. Harris? The nurses won't tell me, and Dr. Sherrill just gives me a lot of medical jargon. Please. Won't you tell me — when can I go home? How much longer do I have to be in here?"

"Well, hon, I can't say. That is, I'm not really on top of your case like Dr. Sherrill. I'm just — "

"Dr. Harris," I interrupted, "you're lying. You know. Tell me."

He replaced the charts, looked serious for a moment, then concentrated on bringing forth his best bedside cheerfulness. "Tell y' what, lass. I'll talk with Dr. Sherrill. I'll have him give y' the whole story in plain English. How's that?"

I smiled. "Better. I mean, I have a right to know, don't I?"

Dr. Harris nodded and pursed his lips as if to say something; then, as if thinking better of it, he merely smiled.

Dick came bursting into the ward later that day. He was wearing a jacket, which was unusual for August.

"I — I've just run up all nine floors!" he gasped.

"Why?" I laughed. "Why didn't you use the elevator?"

"This is why," he replied, opening his jacket. He pulled out a small, lively puppy. It began to climb all over Dick, lying on the floor under my Stryker Frame, licking his face, and barking quietly with a *yip — yip — yip* we thought would alert the entire hospital.

"Sh-h! Quiet, pooch — you want us to get kicked out?" Dick begged.

He put the puppy up by my face. I felt its fuzzy warmth and the wetness of his tongue licking my cheek.

"Oh, Dickie — he's beautiful. I'm glad you brought him."

"I thought I heard something!" a nurse exclaimed in

mock seriousness. "How did you get him past the Gestapo in the lobby?" she grinned.

"I came up the back stairs. You aren't going to turn us in, are you?"

"Who, me?" She bent down and cuddled the puppy, then put him down. "I don't see anything," she said simply and left for other duties.

Dick and I played with the puppy for nearly an hour before being discovered again. He picked up the small dog. "I'll take the stairs again," he said as he got up to leave. "Otherwise they may frisk me every time I come up here!"

We laughed, and Dick left with the puppy hidden beneath his jacket.

*   *   *   *

The next day I was taken down to the laboratory for a bone scan and myelogram. The bone scan was done quickly and smoothly, for it consisted basically of "taking a picture" of my spine. However, the myelogram was not so simple or painless. It meant tapping my spinal cord of its fluid and replacing it with a special dye, using two giant six-inch hypodermic needles. My spinal fluid was drained, pushed out by the dye going in. When the transfer was complete, I was turned upside down and placed in various positions under the fluoroscope while the medics ran their tests. When done, the dye was removed by injecting the spinal fluid back. One side effect of this treatment was a severe headache if some of the fluid was lost or nerve endings (which need the fluid as a lubricant) dried out. There was no medication for this, so I was sedated for several days.

When Dr. Sherrill, the physician in charge of my case, came by later, I accosted him. "Dr. Sherrill, what's wrong with me?"

His reply was even, without inflection, so I had no way of measuring the seriousness of what he said. "Don't you remember, Joni? You have a lesion of the spinal cord at the fourth and fifth cervical levels caused by a fracture-dislocation."

"I broke my neck?"

"Yes."

"But that means I'll die."

"No. Not necessarily," Dr. Sherrill replied. "It means only that it is a very serious accident. The fact that you've survived about four weeks now means you've more than likely passed that crisis."

"You mean you thought I was going to die? Before?"

"You were a badly injured girl. Many people don't survive accidents of this nature."

I thought of Tom and the other man who had died undergoing the same treatment as I was. "I guess I'm lucky," I offered.

"Lucky, indeed. And strong. You have a tremendous will. Now that we've passed this crisis, I want you to concentrate all your will power on getting better. You see, when you're strong enough, I want to perform fusion surgery on you."

"What's that? In plain English, please, Dr. Sherrill."

"Well, it's sort of a repair process. Your spinal cord is severed. We have to fuse the bones back together."

Back together? My mind grabbed at the simple statement and raced with it. *That means I'll get my arms and legs back! That's what Romans 8:28 meant. Dickie was right – things do work together for good. Before long I'll be back on my feet!*

"When do you want to do the surgery?" I asked.

"As soon as possible."

"Great. Let's do it!"

*   *   *   *

I didn't know all that was involved in fusion surgery. I thought that by fusing the bones back together and having the spinal cord healed everything would be the same as before — no more paralysis. But I wasn't really listening carefully.

Following surgery, I was elated to leave the ICU ward and be wheeled into a regular room. *It's a sign I'm getting better,* I thought. *If I wasn't, they'd keep me in ICU.*

Mom and dad, smiling and happy to see me return from the surgery, were in my room, and Dr. Sherrill came by.

"Everything went fine," he said, anticipating our question. "The surgery was a complete success."

There was a collective sigh of relief.

"Now I want you all to concentrate on the next steps of recovery. There is much progress to be made yet. There will be difficult days ahead, Joni. I want you to know it and brace yourself for them. The toughest part of the battle is the psychological aspect. You're fine now. You've been angry, frustrated, afraid. However, you haven't really been depressed. But wait until your friends go off to college. Wait until the novelty of all this wears off. Wait until your friends get other interests and stop coming. Are you ready for that, Joni? If not, better get ready. Because it'll come. Believe me, it'll come."

"I know it'll take time, but I'll get better," I gamely replied. "These things take time — you said so yourself, doctor."

"Yes," dad said. "How much time are we talking about, Dr. Sherrill?"

Mother added her concern, too. "You're talking about Joni's friends going off to college this fall. But I sense you're saying Joni won't be able to. We made a deposit on her tuition for the fall term at Western Maryland University. Should we postpone her entrance until next semester?"

"Uh   at least."

"Really?"

"Mrs. Eareckson, you might as well have them return your deposit. I'm afraid college will be out of the question for Joni."

"Y-you mean — that you don't know how soon Joni will walk again?"

"Walk? I'm afraid you don't understand, Mrs. Eareckson. Joni's injury is permanent. The fusion surgery didn't change that."

The word *permanent* slammed into my consciousness like a bullet.

I could tell that this was also the first time mom and dad had been confronted with the fact of a permanent injury. Either we had all been too naive or the medical people had been too vague in their explanations. Perhaps both.

Silence hung over the room for a few moments. None of us dared react for fear of upsetting and worrying the others.

Dr. Sherrill tried to be encouraging, however. "Joni will never walk again, but we're hoping she'll regain the use of her hands one day. Many people lead useful and constructive lives without being able to walk. Why, they can drive, work, clean house — it's really not a hopeless thing, you know. We're confident she'll be able to get her hands back in time."

Mom had turned her face away, but I knew she was crying.

"Don't worry, mom — dad. There have been lots of times people with broken necks have recovered and walked again. I've heard lots of success stories while I've been here. I'm going to walk again! I know it. I believe God wants me to walk again. He'll help me. Really! I'm going to walk out of here!"

Dr. Sherrill didn't say anything. He put his hand on mom's shoulder, shook hands with daddy, and left. For a long while none of us said anything. Then we began to chat about inconsequential things. Finally my parents left.

I lay in the dim light of the room. I should have been happy — the surgery was successful, I was getting better, and I was now in my own room. But I wasn't happy. Grief, remorse, and depression swept over me like a thick, choking blanket. For the first time since the accident, I wished and prayed I might die.

After nearly an hour, a nurse, Alice, came by. She emptied my catheter bag and rearranged things in my room. Then she went over to the window to adjust the drapes.

"Looks like you'll be getting some visitors," she said.

"Oh?"

"Uh-huh. I see your mom and dad sitting together down in the courtyard outside. They'll probably be up here in a minute."

"No — they've already been here," I replied. I felt tears, hot and salty, spill out of my eyes and roll down my cheeks. My nose became stuffy. I couldn't even cry because I couldn't blow my own nose. I began to sob anyway.

"Hey, what's wrong, Joni?" Alice wiped my face with a tissue. She pulled another from the box. "Here. Blow. Feel better now?"

I smiled. "I'm sorry. Guess I was just thinking of mom and dad down there. Dr. Sherrill just told us that my injury is permanent — that I'll never walk again. I know they're down there talking about it. And crying. And I'm up here crying. It's just too much to handle, I guess."

Alice ran the back of her hand along the side of my face. Her concern, her gesture, felt good. It was reassuring and comforting to feel something..

"I'm going to walk out of here, Alice. God will help me. You'll see."

Alice nodded and smiled.

*   *   *   *

During the weeks following surgery, I didn't get stronger as I had vowed. Still fed intravenously or by liquids, my weight began to drop. The thought of solid food made me nauseous, and I just couldn't eat food brought on trays to my room. I could only drink grape juice. The nurses stocked up on it and brought me glasses to sip.

One day a stranger in a hospital uniform came into my room. "I'm Willie, the chef," he explained. "I came to see why you don't like my food," he added.

"Oh, it's not your food. I just get sick thinking about food in general," I apologized.

"What did you like best? Before the accident, I mean?"

"Before? Well, my favorite foods were steak —
baked potatoes — "

"Vegetable?"

"Oh, I don't know. Corn, I guess."

"Salad?"

"I liked Caesar salads."

"Well, let's see what we can do." Then he left.

That evening a nurses' aide brought my tray as
usual. As she lifted the cover, I saw a big steak, huge
baked potato with butter and sour cream, sweet corn, and
magnificent Caesar salad. But when she put the tray
down in front of me, somehow the smell made me nauseous again.

"Please. Take it away. I'm sorry — I just can't eat
it."

She shook her head and took the tray back, and I
turned away in frustration and sadness.

I never knew whether the nausea was typical or just
a side effect of some medication. I was used to the
hallucinations by now, and I believe even some of my
dreams, or nightmares, were drug-induced. Lately I
had sensed ugly "beings" standing around my hospital
bed, waiting to carry me away, and this daydream or
nightmare or hallucination, whatever it was, depressed
me further. I couldn't really see them, but I knew they
were there — terrible and fierce, waiting for me to die —
or maybe just fall asleep. I fought sleep for fear of being
carried off by them.

I was glad when visitors came, for to some extent,
their presence kept me in touch with reality and gave me
something to look forward to. But I never really knew how
difficult it was for them to come back day after day.

When friends came to visit for the first time, they
were awkward and uncertain of how to act in a hospital
room. As they began to be somewhat at ease, they all
asked the same questions.

"What does it feel like?"

"Does it hurt?"

"How do you go to the bathroom?"

Many visitors were squeamish and uncomfortable; some were particularly upset to see the tongs pressing into my skull. It often seemed they had more difficulty coping with my situation than I did.

One day two girl friends from high school came to visit. They had not seen me since before the accident, and I was as unprepared for their reaction as they were. They came into the room and slowly looked around at the Stryker Frame and other paraphernalia. Then they stopped hesitantly beside me. I watched out of the corner of my eye as they came toward me.

"Hi," I smiled. "I'm sorry I can't turn my head to see you, but if you'll — "

"Oh, Joni!" choked one of the girls.

"Oh, my God — " whispered the other.

There was an awkward silence for a moment — then I heard them run for the door. Outside the door, I heard one girl retch and vomit while her friend began to sob loudly.

I felt a twinge of horror sweep over me. No one else had acted that unusual. Were they particularly squeamish around hospitals — or was there something else?

For awhile I didn't want to know. Then a few days later when Jackie came to visit, I looked up at her and said, "Jackie, bring me a mirror."

She had been reading some cards and other mail and looked up abruptly. "Why?" she asked.

"I want you to get me a mirror."

"Uh — okay. I'll bring one next time I come."

"No. I mean now. Get one from the nurse."

"Why don't we wait. I'll bring you your pretty dresser set from home."

"Jackie!" I was getting angry at her. "Bring me a mirror! Now!"

She slowly edged toward the door and was back shortly with a mirror. Her hands were shaking, and her eyes blinked nervously as she held it up before me.

I screamed and Jackie jumped, nearly dropping the mirror. "It's ghastly!

"Oh, God, how can You do this to me?" I prayed through tears. "What have You done to me?"

The figure in the mirror seemed scarcely human. As I stared at my own reflection, I saw two eyes, darkened and sunk into the sockets, bloodshot and glassy. My weight had dropped from 125 to 80, so that I appeared to be little more than a skeleton covered by yellow, jaundiced skin. My shaved head only accented my grotesque skeletal appearance. As I talked, I saw my teeth, black from the effects of medication.

I, too, felt like vomiting.

Jackie took away the mirror and began to cry with me. "I'm sorry, Joni," she sobbed, "I didn't want you to see."

"Please take it away. I never want to look in a mirror again!

"Jackie — I can't take it any more. I'm dying, Jackie. Look at me. I'm almost dead now. Why do they let me suffer like this?"

"I — I don't know, Joni."

"Jackie, you've got to help me. They're keeping me alive. It's not right. I'm dying anyway. Why can't they just let me die? Jackie — please — you've got to help," I pleaded.

"But how, Joni?"

"I don't know. Give me something — you know — an overdose of pills?"

"You mean you want me to kill you?" Jackie asked wide-eyed.

"Yes — I mean no — you won't be killing me. You'll just be helping me die sooner. Look, I'm already dying. I'm suffering. Can't you help me end the suffering? If I could move, I'd do it myself!" I was angry and frustrated. "Please — cut my wrists — there's no feeling. I'd have no pain. I'll die peaceful, Jackie. Please! Do something."

Jackie began to sob. "I can't, Joni. I just can't!"

I begged her, "Jackie, if you care for me at all, you've got to help. I'm dying anyway — can't you see? Look at me! Just look at me."

"Joni, you don't know what you're asking. I just can't. Maybe you *would* be better off, I don't know. I'm so mixed up! I want to help. I love you more than I love anyone, and it kills me to see you suffer like this. But — but I can't do it!"

I didn't say anything more then. Several other times, though, in similar spells of depression and frustration, I begged Jackie to help me commit suicide. I was angry because I couldn't do it by myself.

I fantasized about how it could be done. Pills would be easiest, but the nurses would find me and pump my stomach. I could have Jackie slash my wrists. Since I had no feeling there, I'd have no pain. I could hide them under the sheets and — no, that wouldn't work either. All I could do was wait and hope for some hospital accident to kill me.

Jackie became more conscious of my appearance after these bouts with depression. She tried to help me "look good" to people and to interest me in things that might take my mind off my situation.

"You'll be better soon, Joni," she promised. "Remember, the Lord says He will never allow us to suffer more than we can humanly bear."

"Oh, yeah?" I grunted.

The medication and paralysis also left me with an acute sensitivity to light and sound. I made Jackie and the nurses keep the shades and blinds drawn and the door shut to keep out light and noise. Dr. Harris said it was evidence of nerves beginning to heal, but I was dreadfully discomforted by it. I could even hear conversations clearly from adjoining rooms. The usual hospital routine turned into a harsh, discordant cacophony.

One hot summer day, Jackie was moving a fan for me, and she accidentally dropped it. It sounded like a painful explosion going off inside my head as it clattered on the tile floor.

"Jackie!" I screamed and cursed at her. The ugly words which came out of my mouth were strange and obscene, dredged up from some dark recess of my mind. I called her awful names.

Then guilt washed over me. "I'm sorry, Jackie. It's so easy to cave in." I cried softly. "I know God must have some purpose in all this. Please call Dickie before you go. I need him. Tell him to come up tonight."

Jackie nodded and started to leave.

"Jackie — wait. There's something I have to say before you go."

She stood near me. "Jackie, you're such a close friend — I'm taking you for granted. I yell at you all the time — especially since I can't scream at anyone else! I feel like being mad at God, at mom and dad, at Dickie. Y'know? It kinda gets to me sometimes, and I have to let off steam. But you're the only one I can safely scream at. Mom and dad are already suffering so much — I have to make a special effort to be pleasant when they come. It isn't fair for me to be critical, demanding, and mean to them. And I can't take a chance on losing Dick by taking things out on him. I need him; I don't want to lose him, maybe forever, by hurting him now. So, Jackie, I'm sorry. You've been my scapegoat. You get the brunt of every ugly emotion I let go."

Jackie smiled warmly and shrugged. "That's okay, Joni. I know you don't really mean it. Besides," she grinned, "what are friends for?"

She came over, smoothed my hospital gown, and kissed me on the forehead. "I'll call Dick for you."

Dick came by the hospital later. Quietly I lay there listening to the comforting words of Scripture he read to me from a J. B. Phillips New Testament paraphrase. Many of the verses were alive with contemporary meaning.

"Listen to this, Joni," Dick said excitedly. " 'When all kinds of trials and temptations crowd into your lives, my brothers, don't resent them as intruders, but welcome them as friends! Realize that they come to test your faith and to produce in you the quality of endurance' " (James 1:2-4).

"What do you suppose it means, Dickie?"

"I think it means just what it says — that God has allowed your accident to happen for a purpose, not as an intrusion in your life, but to test your faith and spiritual endurance."

"Oh, wow! Have I ever been letting the Lord down."

"Listen to the rest of it, Joni. 'And if, in the process, any of you does not know how to meet any particular problem he has only to ask God — who gives generously to all men without making them feel foolish or guilty.'"

"My problem is one *I* can't meet. Let's ask God to heal me. Just like it says."

Dick put the book down and began. "Father, we thank You for Your care and concern. We thank You for Your Word, the Bible, and the promises You have there for us. Your Word says, 'If any of you does not know how to meet any particular problem, he has only to ask God.' Well, Lord, we're asking — please hear our prayers, in Jesus' name, amen."

I prayed next. "Lord Jesus, I'm sorry I haven't been looking more to You for help. I've never thought of my accident before as something for testing my faith. But I can see how that's happened. Lord, just like Your Word says, I believe my accident came to test my faith and endurance, but I also feel that You really want me healed. Thank You for this lesson. With Your help, I'm going to trust You. Thank You that even this accident 'works' together for good. I pray that others around me will see You through me. In Your name I pray, amen."

After that, I began to see more positive aspects about my accident. During the following days I shared with nurses, doctors, and visitors the thought that God had allowed my accident merely to test my faith and endurance. "Now, with that lesson learned, I can trust Him to get me back on my feet. You'll see!"

I took this attitude with everything.

The doctor told dad, "You should know that your insurance probably won't begin to cover the expenses of Joni's accident. Her hospital bills will likely be $30,000 or more before she leaves."

I said simply, "Don't worry, God will provide us with what we need."

When Dr. Sherrill explained, "Joni, paralysis is generally a lot harder on an athletic person than ordinary people. I want you to know that when depression sets in, you'll really have a struggle with it."

"God will help me," I replied glibly.

When a nurse commented, "I was reading about your accident. You know, if your break had occurred an inch or less lower, you'd still have the use of your arms. Sad, isn't it?"

I answered, "Yes. But if the break was an inch higher, I'd be dead. God knows best, doesn't He?"

Just after Labor Day, Dick stopped by with a present. My room was overflowing with stuffed animals, posters, pictures, cards, and other get-well momentos. One of them was a green and white plush bear which I doused with British Sterling shaving lotion and named after Dick. The familiar scent reminded and reassured me of Dick when he was absent.

This time, Dick gave me a huge study Bible — one with print large enough to read when it was laid on the floor below my Stryker Frame. I could read it by myself if someone turned the pages. In the front, he wrote:

> "To my dearest Joni, with hopes that Christ will always remain in our relationship, and that Christ might give us the patience to wait for each other. With all kinds of love,
>
> Dick
>
> Sept. 9, 1967   Romans 8:28"

Not long after Labor Day, Dick, Jackie, and all my friends went away to college. Dick hitchhiked back as often as possible to be with me. I didn't know how difficult this was for him — or that his grades suffered as a result of his concern for me. I just took it for granted that he should be there. In my selfish little world, I didn't care how he managed it; I just wanted him to be there with me. After all, I needed him. Without knowing it, I began to use my accident as a device to keep him interested. I even resorted to blackmail one evening.

"Hi, Joni," Dick grinned as he bent over to kiss me.

"Where have you been? It's nearly eight o'clock."

"Sorry. I couldn't get away. How was your day?"

"You said you'd be here by six, and it's now eight. You can only stay here a half-hour now before you have to leave. What kind of visit is that?" I fumed.

"Joni, I said I'm sorry. I couldn't get away." Dick was getting defensive, and I didn't want him to get angry.

"Dickie, my day is absolutely miserable without you. Last night I dreamed you left me for another girl."

"I'd never do that — "

"Oh, promise me, Dickie. Tell me you love me and that you'll never leave me."

"You know how much I care for you, hon."

"Tell me. Tell me."

"I love you." Dick said simply. I could tell he didn't want to say it. Not because he didn't care for me deeply — I know he did. Rather, he resented my telling him to say it. He wanted to tell me in his own way, in his own time. But he smiled and added, as if to make the statement spontaneous, "I've loved you for a long time, Joni. If you'd waited five minutes, I'd have told you again — without prompting."

"But I needed to hear you say it now, Dickie."

"All right. I love you. I love you. I love you." Each time he said it, he bent over and kissed me.

"Oh, Dickie. I love you, too. Won't it be great when I'm able to leave here?"

"I'm praying it'll be soon. Boy, this hitchhiking sure wrecks my study habits."

"It may be a long time."

"Oh? Did you hear something today?"

"It'll be several months of rehabilitation. Maybe a year."

"Oh, wow."

"Dickie, I'm scared. I can take it if you're with me. You have to help me. But I can't do it without you. If you leave me, I'll die. I know it. I won't be able to live without you. Promise me you won't leave me."

"Of course."

"If you really love me, promise you'll be with me forever — "

"Sure," he said, glancing down.

"First I'll get my hands back. Then I'll walk. Then we can go to college together," I promised.

"Right," whispered Dick.

"How is college? Is it really neat?"

"Oh, it's fine. Really a lot tougher than high school, though," said Dick. "A lot tougher."

"Maybe because you're doing so much. How's the team doing?" I asked.

"The team? Oh, just fine, I guess. First game is Friday."

"Are you all ready for it?" I asked excitedly.

"I'm not playing," said Dick simply.

"Not playing? Why?"

"I lost my football scholarship."

"But why?"

"Look, it doesn't matter."

"Oh, Dickie, I'm sorry." *It's because he has to visit me so much – he has no time to study*, I told myself.

"It's all right. We've still got time for that. Want me to read something from the Bible?"

"Not tonight, Dickie. I'm tired. And you'll have to go in a minute. Just hug me and kiss me before you go."

He bent over me and held my chin in his hand. He kissed me softly, lingeringly. "I love you," he whispered. "I'll wait forever for you — you know that. Remember that always. I'll always be here."

When he left, I cried bitterly. I felt cheap and selfish. I had put Dick over a barrel. What choice did he have? Could he say how he really felt: "Joni, we're still too young to know if we should get married. We don't know God's will for the future. Let's just play it by ear. You know you can always count on me. I care for you deeply." I'm sure that's what he would have said. But that wasn't strong enough for my frayed emotions. And Dick was too sensitive to hurt my feelings — especially after the accident — so he said what I wanted to hear.

Now I had driven a wedge into our relationship. I had forced feelings and commitments before they were ripe. I began to mistrust all my own motives.

"I'll make it right," I promised the Lord in my prayers that night. "I'll do everything I can to be worthy of Dick's love. I'll do everything possible to walk again. Then he won't have to love me because of the accident but because he wants to. Things will be better. That's what I want, Lord. Please — please. . . ."

* * * *

When the hospital therapist came by the next day, I remembered Jason's instructions: "You gotta fight." PT — physical therapy was the first step in actual rehabilitation. I decided to give it everything I had.

The therapist fastened my arms in slings and began to explain the process.

"Your fracture was at the fourth and fifth cervical level, as you know. At the first level are nerves for vital organs — heart and lungs. People who have breaks at this first level seldom live.

"The second and third levels control neck muscles and head movement," she continued. "At the fourth and fifth levels, quadriplegia — like your case — generally results. The sixth level controls the pectoral and arm muscles. Now, you have feelings in your shoulders, upper arm, and chest just above your breasts. That means that maybe you can train other muscles — muscles in the back and shoulders — to compensate for certain arm muscles you've lost."

"Is that what the doctors mean about getting the use of my hands back?" I asked her.

"Partly. Your chart indicates you've got about 50 percent use of your biceps — those are the upper arm muscles that move the arm in its fullest range of movements. We won't know until we get into therapy just how much you'll be able to do. We'll have to train new muscles to do motor movements for the ones you've lost."

"All right, let's try it," I said.

"First, try to lift your arm by using the muscles of your back, neck, and shoulders. Just move it to begin with," she instructed.

I tried. Nothing happened. I closed my eyes to concentrate more intensely. I felt the muscles tense and vibrate, but they seemed independent of my will. I could not get them to move.

"Keep trying. You'll get it," the therapist urged.

I gritted my teeth and tried again. Nothing.

"C'mon, Joni. Try again," she insisted.

"Don't you think I'm trying?" I snapped and swore for emphasis.

"It's a matter of directing new muscles to do the work of the old ones. Don't try to lift your arm with the old movements. Think of how the muscles in the arm are hooked up to the ligaments and bones — here." She showed me diagrams in a book and traced the lines on my own arm. "Try to get movement from these muscles. Just twist or flex your back and try to move your arm in the process."

I tried once more as she pointed to the spot. For more than ten minutes I exerted all my will power and strength. Finally my arm rose less than an inch and flopped back limply.

"Beautiful! Great! Once more," she instructed. "Put all your energy and concentration into lifting that arm and holding it up."

Using all the strength I could gather, I tried again. After several tense moments of agonizing effort, my arm raised once more — this time about an inch off the table — and strained against the slings fastened to it.

"Again!" she ordered.

"I can't. It hurts. It's too tiring. I have to rest first," I begged. Nearly a half-hour had gone by, and all I had done was move my arm about an inch two times.

"All right, Joni. You can see it is going to be hard work. We have a lot to do before you can really begin rehabilitation. But soon we'll have you strong enough to leave here for Greenoaks," she smiled.

"Greenoaks?"

"Yes. Greenoaks Rehabilitation Center," she explained. "Dr. Sherrill will tell you all about it. That's the next step. It's a hospital specializing in motor-damaged cases."

"A rehabilitation center? Oh, yeah — I remember now. That's where I'll learn to walk!"

The therapist smiled, unfastened the slings, and stood up. "Good luck, Joni. I'll work with you again tomorrow. Let's get you ready for Greenoaks!"

Four

For nearly a month, I concentrated on getting prepared for Greenoaks. That was where I would learn to walk and begin life again. When word came that they had a place for me, everyone was excited. The nurses and doctors all came by to wish me well on this step toward rehabilitation.

"Well, lassie, y'behave yourself now. No wild parties and carryin' on," Dr. Harris teased, "or we'll have to come and get you and bring you back here."

"Oh, no you won't!" I exclaimed, "you'll never get me back here — you guys have plenty of sick people to work with. Well, one of these days, I might come back," I amended, "but it'll be on my own two feet — and I'll take you to McDonald's for lunch."

"It's a date, lassie," Dr. Harris grinned. He squeezed my shoulder, winked, and left.

Two nurses — Anita (my favorite) and Alice — helped take down the pictures and posters and pack away all the things I had accumulated — several boxes — during my three-and-a-half month stay at the hospital.

Finally the orderlies came in to transfer me to the

ambulance waiting downstairs to take me to Greenoaks. As they wheeled me through the outside double doors at the ground level, a slight rush of beautiful, sweet-smelling, outdoor air tickled my nostrils and the bright sunlight was everywhere.

"Oh, wow! Wait just a minute, please," I asked the two orderlies. "Do you smell that air?" I said excitedly.

"Polluted!" snorted one of the guys good-naturedly.

"Oh, it's beautiful!" I breathed deeply of its rich and, to me, heady fragrance.

"Hey, you're gonna get high on oxygen," teased one of the men. They eased my stretcher into the ambulance, shut the doors, and we began the drive to Greenoaks.

I couldn't help contrasting this ambulance drive with my last one. Then the trees had been green, the grass and flowers lush and gorgeous. The air had been hot and humid, the people dressed in summer clothes.

Today, the air was crisp and cool. The stores were decorated for Halloween and fall sales. The trees were gold, red, and orange — the landscape reflected the full variety of autumn colors and textures.

An entire season had passed by while I was in the hospital! It was a strange feeling, but it did not stay to disturb me. The excitement and beauty of the ride was much too thrilling to waste worrying about a lost summer. I let the warm sun bathe my face through the window, and the driver kept his window rolled down so the fresh air could come in and sweep over me. It was such a pleasurable experience that I almost cried with joy.

As we approached Greenoaks, I became even more excited. Greenoaks. Even the name had a pleasant ring to it. In my mind I pictured a big, colonial structure with tall, white pillars overlooking sweeping green lawns shaded by huge green oak trees.

When we pulled into the driveway, however, I could see that it looked nothing like this. It was a sprawling, low brick building, more like an industrial park, office complex, or factory.

"Well, here we are," said the driver.

"Yeah," I said slowly.

"Anything wrong?"

"Uh — no. I guess not," I said sheepishly. "I suppose any place you build up in your mind doesn't live up to your expectations. Y'know?"

He nodded, then added, "Don't worry — they do good work here. I think you'll like it. Quite a few girls your age here. You should hit it off swell."

"I hope so," I replied apprehensively. As he wheeled me down the corridor to my assigned ward, I looked around and into open doors of various rooms. It was quiet, like the hospital. No one was "cured" — *walking*.

I saw people slouched in wheelchairs, encased in Stryker Frames, or lying in beds. The halls seemed dark and depressing, with people lined up in wheelchairs. It was an old institution, badly in need of decorating.

By the time we got to my room, I was discouraged.

Mom and dad were there to meet me. They had signed me in and cared for the billing details and other business. They tried to cheer me up, but as soon as I was as comfortable as possible, they excused themselves. I had seen this reaction before — at City Hospital when they were told of the permanence of my injury. I knew they were again on the verge of breaking down and didn't want me to see their tears and disappointment. They left, promising, "We'll be back soon as possible, darling."

I looked around at my room when they left. Four other girls shared the small ward with me. I decided to introduce myself. "Hi. I'm Joni Eareckson," I began.

"Joni Eareckson!" I heard my name repeated contemptuously, followed by a string of obscenities. "That's all I heard at City Hospital — Joni this, Joni that. I could puke!"

Stunned by the bitter voice, I recovered enough to smile and say, "Oh, I didn't know I had a fan club here."

The ice was broken. The others laughed. "You'll have to excuse Ann," explained one girl. "She's new here, too. She came to City Hospital after you, and I guess she wasn't quite the model patient you were. They did an awful lot of comparing her with you. I'm Betty —

Betty Jackson. The girl in the bed over there is Denise Walters."

"Hi. Pardon me if I don't get up."

"Yeah, I know the *un*-feeling," I wisecracked, adding, "Nice to meet you, Denise."

"And this is Betty, too," said Betty Jackson, pointing with a flop of a useless arm, "Betty Glover. They call me B.J. to tell us apart." Betty Glover was a pretty, petite black girl who looked much younger than the rest of us.

"Hi, Betty," I smiled.

Betty looked up and nodded slightly.

"I'm here because of a broken neck — like you," B.J. explained. "Betty has a blood clot on her spine. They're working on her to see why she's paralyzed. And Denise is here because she has M.S."

"M.S.?" I asked ignorantly.

"Multiple sclerosis."

I regretted asking. I recalled hearing about M.S. in the hospital. *It's a fatal disease. Denise will probably be dead before she reaches her twentieth birthday*, I thought, shivering inwardly, and wondered how she maintained her gracious and open attitude.

"And in this cor-nah," clowned B.J., "is Ann Wilson, whose mouth you've already met. Ann is in charge of b _ _ _ _ _ _ _ ."

"Aw, go — " Ann cursed. She took a cigarette from her lips and threw it at Denise. It landed harmlessly on the tile floor.

"Well, now you've met us. You ready for this marriage?" asked B.J.

"I — I guess so, yeah," I stammered. *Except for Ann and that smoke*, I thought to myself.

Ann had lit up another cigarette. In the hospital, I had discouraged people from smoking around me. In Greenoaks, many of the patients smoked. To me, smoking was ugly, smelly, and something I wanted other people to do only in their own homes or rooms — not around me. I hated the choking smoke and acrid smell. But now I could claim only one-fifth of this room. There wasn't anything to do but get used to the smoke and make the best of the situation.

I tried the one ploy I knew and said to Ann, "You know, that stuff causes lung cancer. It'll kill you.

She looked squarely at me and replied in even tones, "Why do you think I'm doing it?"

But Ann wasn't nearly as difficult and contrary as my first impressions of her. I could see a lot of my own attitudes of bitterness and resentment in her. *A few weeks ago, I was going through the same depression and despondency,* I remembered. I wanted to kill myself, too. Ann was more confused than anything else. She used anger to lash out because she didn't know what else to do. I decided to try and get to know her better.

During the next few days, I got an even closer look at Greenoaks. Patients from every age, economic, occupational, and racial background were housed in the four wings of the institution. They consisted of amputees, paraplegics, quadriplegics, polio victims, and those suffering from muscular dystrophy, multiple sclerosis, and other diseases affecting the motor and nervous systems.

"How come there are so many new people — mostly guys our age?" I asked B.J.

"Broken necks. Most broken necks happen in summer with swimming and diving accidents. They usually spend a couple months in city hospitals and then come here for rehab," B.J. explained.

I made a mental note of the way she abbreviated the word *rehabilitation.* I listened for other such "inside" or slang terms used by the girls so I would not sound so much like a greenhorn.

"How many broken neck cases are new?" I asked.

"Oh, maybe ten, fifteen."

"How long have you been here, B.J.?"

"Two years," she answered.

Two years! I recoiled inwardly at the thought. *Two years — and she's still paralyzed and in bed like me!* The fact that *I* might be here that long really depressed me. I was silent for a long while.

That night as I lay in my Stryker Frame trying to

sleep, I was troubled by the old attitudes and bitterness that had made me so despondent at the hospital. I tried to pray and couldn't. I tried to think of some promises from God's Word to encourage me. Nothing seemed reassuring.

Seemingly the other girls had adjusted. They were chatting quietly, waiting for "lights out." Except for Ann. She was complaining loudly, punctuating her objections with salty language. I decided that even if I had to be in an institution the rest of my life, I'd be pleasant — at least on the surface — and not like Ann. She had absolutely no friends on the outside. And inside, people treated her in kind. No one tried to understand her or make friends with her.

I need to have my friends, or I'll lose my mind, I said to myself, so I promised myself never to lose my cool with mom, dad, Jackie, or the others when they came to visit. No matter how bitter I was, I wouldn't let it show.

"That's a good idea," observed B.J. when I told her about my thoughts the next day. "In here, everyone's the same. So you won't find much sympathy here. In fact, you'd be smart not to make many friends here."

"Why?" I wondered.

"It's an ivory tower. Everyone here is the same — give or take an arm or two — so it's comfortable. You get out for visits home when you have enough sitting-up time, but you can't wait to get back. It's easier to be here with people like us. No hassling about braces, wheelchairs, and stuff. It's hard to leave here. The people on the street think because your legs are paralyzed, your brain must be, too. They treat 'cha like a dummy. So everybody always comes back here complaining and comparing injuries, but content to stay because they feel at home here. You'll be the same if you make all your friends here. Just because it's *easier* to be in an ivory tower doesn't mean it's better. It isn't. I know. I've been here two years. Whatever you do, keep your friends on the outside!"

Jay seemed to sense my emotional needs in that regard. She not only came often herself, but often

rounded up old school chums to visit. I especially remember Jay and several friends dressing up in costumes
and coming over on Halloween night. There was no
bending of rules here, though. Unlike City Hospital
nurses, Greenoaks' staff rigidly enforced visiting hours.
Promptly at eight o'clock, Jay and our friends were asked
to leave.

My days became dull routine, brightened only by
my visitors. I was confined to bed because of bedsores. A
nurse would feed me in the morning and empty my
catheter bag. Then she'd check the round mirror above
my head to see that it was focused for me to watch TV.

About noon, I'd be fed and "emptied" again. And
more TV in the afternoon. Mornings were the game
shows. Afternoons, the soap operas. At evening, another
meal and catheter emptying followed by more television
watching until "lights out." Each new day was a boring
and monotonous extension of the previous day — eat,
watch TV, sleep — in an unbreaking, sickening cycle.

I had to learn to eat and drink my food quickly. The
staff people were always busy, too busy to linger with
those who dawdled with their meals. They were also too
busy to really do more than care for our immediate
physical needs. If my nose itched, I'd have to wait until
Jay or a staff person was nearby. My hair was growing
back and became tangled, matted, dirty, and snowing
dandruff because no one had time to wash it.

One day when Jay came for a visit, she asked,
"What's that horrible smell?"

"What smell?" I asked.

"Ugh! It's your hair. When did they wash it last?"
Jay demanded.

"Over a month ago. At City Hospital," I replied.

"It's awful! It stinks, it's so bad! I've got to do
something about that!" she exclaimed. Jay checked, got
a basin and soap, and improvised a means for sham-
pooing my hair.

"Oh, it feels so good!" I exclaimed

"Me next!" called out Denise. "Wash my hair,
please, Jay."

"Then me," echoed B.J. and Betty together. So, a regular hair wash and set, along with brushing, became Jay's duty to the five of us every week, until "regulations" put an end to her efforts.

With my hair now growing out and sometimes even combed, I began to take a little interest in my appearance. The side effects of the medication had slackened somewhat by now, too, and I didn't seem quite so grotesque. However, I was still thin and underweight, and my bones bulged through my skin causing open, ugly bedsores.

Diana White, a friend from high school and *Young Life*, began to visit me regularly. She was a sensitive, caring Christian girl, with a positive, out-going personality. She always seemed happy and cheerful. Yet, she was practical as well as optimistic. Her attitude was not glib, happy-go-lucky naiveté. Rather, she encountered difficulty and pessimism with her own strong personality. She had an innate spirit of helpfulness and won instant acceptance with people. Diana's wide face, dark hair, and eyes lighted up when she talked, and the corners of her mouth curled up in a smile, making me feel brighter, better.

I appreciated her visits more and more because Jackie — now facing some inner turmoil of her own — no longer came as frequently to see me. Diana's encouragement and reading from God's Word also filled the void created by the fact that Dick's studies prevented him from coming as often. Jason began to drift out of my life, too. From others, I heard that he was dating a girl he had met at college and seemed serious about her.

I was grateful when P.T. — physical therapy — became a part of the daily routine, for it offered an additional element of variety to my life.

At first the physical therapist, Barbara Marshall, came to my room to exercise my paralyzed limbs. After a few weeks, I was taken to the P.T. center for two hours of therapy every day. My first impression of this big room was that it resembled a strange torture chamber. There were bizarre machines and devices for stretching, pulling, and bending useless arms, legs, and bodies. But as strange as this room appeared, it had positive overtones for me — I was going to learn to walk like the others I saw moving with crutches and walkers.

Joe Leroy, a brawny therapy aide with great patience, took me to the P.T. room to show me what would happen when the therapist put my limbs through the full range of potential movement to keep them from becoming atrophied.

"Look," he encouraged, "all this flat-on-your-back ballet really does have a purpose." Joe then proceeded to explain how twisting, bending, and stretching my legs, arms and limp body in arcs, circles, and all kinds of angles would help me.

"It keeps your muscles elastic," Joe explained.

"But I can't feel anything. Why does it matter if they get stiff?" I asked.

"Makes problems for the blood — circulation gets bad. Also, when your muscles go, your body gets stiff, your limbs shrivel up, and your body gets all twisted up," Joe said as he pointed to other patients being pulled, pushed, and lifted.

The physical therapists worked with me twenty minutes each day, putting elasticity back into my muscles, even though they would never function again. Next, they began to work with me in order to get me out of my Stryker Frame and into a regular bed.

Then came grueling exercises to try to enable me to sit up. They fastened me to a tilt-board and lifted my head and lowered my legs. As they slowly raised me past the horizontal position, I felt blood rush from my head and waves of nausea sweep over me.

"Wait. Don't go any higher. I can't take it," I cried.

Even just a few seconds with my head elevated was too much after nearly six months in a horizontal position.

"Oh, Joe," I sobbed, "I thought I was going to faint! Won't I ever be able to sit up?"

"Sure, Joni. Just takes time. We only had you elevated about 45 degrees. We'll try again for a little bit longer. When you can take it for several minutes, we'll increase the angle of the tilt-board. By Thanksgiving you should be sitting up in a chair," Joe said brightly.

Earl, another aide, nodded and said, "You see, your body is so used to lyin' flat that your circulation has adapted to this position." Earl punctuated his explanation with wide, sweeping arm gestures. "When we raise your head, the blood leaves your head, and you feel like you're gonna black out. But if we do it slow 'n easy, your heart will 'remember' and begin to do its job again. Your circulation will pick up and blood will be pumped to your brain again."

So we worked out longer and longer each day until I could "sit up" on the tilt-board without blacking out or getting nauseous.

We took inventory of my muscle capability and feeling. Doctors and therapists determined I had full feelings in my head, neck, and shoulders to the collarbones. There was a slight tingling sensation in my upper arms and chest, making it feel as if these parts of my body were asleep.

Diana came by after I was making progress in P.T. and offered her encouragement. Her optimism was contagious. Each time she came to visit, she'd have new encouragement from the Bible. "Listen," she exclaimed, "it's from John 16:24: 'I assure you that whatever you ask the Father he will give you in my name. Up to now you have asked nothing in my name; ask now, and you will receive, that your joy may be overflowing.' Isn't that great?"

"Yeah, it really is. Hey, maybe God is doing something special. Did you hear about our church?" I said.

"Church?" Diana asked. "No. What's happening?"

"Our church is having an all-night prayer service for me. They're going to pray for my healing and recovery," I explained.

"Oh, wow. That's neat! 'Ask now, and you will receive,'" Diana repeated.

I was further encouraged because my P.T. had by now brought a tingling feeling to my fingers. While they were still numb and paralyzed, I could feel a remote sensation in them. I knew God was beginning to heal me.

On the night of the prayer service at church, friends from high school, teachers, parents of friends, and friends of friends crowded into the Bishop Cummings Reformed Episcopal Church. And I went to sleep that night expecting to awake the next morning fully healed.

It didn't happen that way of course. So I rationalized that the Lord was testing our faith and that the healing process and full recovery would come slowly and not in some sudden, supernatural way.

When Diana, Jay, my parents and *Young Life* friends came by for a visit, I gave the outward impression that everything was under control, hiding my disappointment and impatience.

"The Lord's going to heal me," I promised them. "Let's keep praying and trusting."

"Oh, Joni," someone would gush, "you sure are brave. I wish I had your faith."

I'd smile sweetly and pray under my breath for God to hurry up and heal me.

Five

By December I was still weak, thin, and covered with bedsores, but my physical therapy gave me enough sitting-up time so I could go home for one day. I chose Christmas day and began to get excited planning for it. The night after they told me I could go home for a day, I was too thrilled to sleep. I lay in the darkness of my room and tried to recall all the memories of my last Christmas before the accident — walking in the snow with Dick, Christmas Eve at the cathedral, making angels in the snow, drinking hot chocolate beside the fireplace, singing carols as I played my guitar. What would it be like this year?

Christmas Day finally came! Jay helped the nurse dress me for the trip home. I wore the pretty dark suit I had bought on the trip our family had taken out West just weeks before my accident; it hung on me like a sack. Jay also brought me a lovely blond wig to wear over my own hair which was still not long enough to style.

Dad drove up to the door and waited while Joe and Earl carried me to the car. They instructed my family on how a quadriplegic should ride in a car.

"It never occurred to me that just riding in a car is dangerous," I said, adding, "unless, of course, we crash."

"You don't have to be in a wreck to get hurt," Joe cautioned. "You see, a quad can't sit up alone. If the car swerves, stops suddenly, or just turns a corner, you'll be carried by momentum. You'll spill — maybe crack your head on the door or smash your face on the dashboard or windshield, if you're sitting up front." He explained how to use the car's shoulder harness to strap me in but also cautioned to be aware of holding on to me, especially on turns, starts, and stops.

Nothing happened on the way home, although the drive seemed exciting and full of interesting little pleasures. *It's winter now*, I thought. *Two whole seasons have slipped by since I was home.*

"Well, we're almost there now," observed Jay as the car turned at the familiar triangle intersection. I looked up the street — the high school, the house of my piano teacher, the drugstore — everything as I remembered it. A twinge of homesickness swept over me.

In a few minutes, we had driven up the steep avenue in front of my folks' home and pulled into the driveway in back. Dad and Jay gingerly lifted me from the car and carried me inside.

The feelings of homesickness were real by now. The house was decorated for the holidays, and a big, fragrant pine tree had been set up in the dining room where I was to stay.

Mom had somehow obtained a hospital bed and set it up in the dining room. I thought of my old room, just above this one, keeper of so many of my secret thoughts, prayers, and hopes. Of course, my family couldn't carry me up the narrow, twisting staircase to my old room so, for this one day, the dining room would be my room.

Mom had pushed the huge dining room table alongside the wall to make the room more comfortable. Dad must have known when he built the house that we'd entertain a lot, for the room was huge — two or three times the usual dining room size, about eighteen by twenty-five feet — with a large table able to seat fourteen with ease.

A crackling fire in the stone fireplace, beautiful and fragrant Christmas decorations, candles, and lights filled the room with happiness. It was almost too much for my senses. The smells, sights, and sounds were intoxicating. During my hospital stay and confinement at Greenoaks, my spirit had suffered as well as my body, for my spirit had suffered sensory deprivation. Now the room reeled as all of these sweet sensations assaulted my brain in a feast of pleasure.

I was able to sit up only a little while before tiring, so the hospital bed proved useful. I half-sat and half-lay on the bed. Dressed in the suit and blond wig, I looked "almost human," but I was still self-conscious about my appearance. Especially my legs. It seemed to me they were sticking out awkwardly, disgustingly.

"Please, will you cover me, mom?" I asked.

"Are you cold, dear?"

"No. I just want to be covered. I look awful."

"Nonsense," she replied. "You look lovely. Doesn't she, Jay?"

"Of course," answered my sister.

"But I still want to be covered. Bring that brown blanket and put it over my legs. I don't want people coming over to stare. Please!" I was insistent.

"All right, Joni. As you wish," sighed mom, as she spread the blanket over my legs and tucked it in. The real reason I wanted my legs covered wasn't because others would be offended by my useless limbs. Rather, it was because they were a constant reminder to me of how different this Christmas was. I couldn't bear to look at them.

Dick, along with friends and family, came to visit that day, and the time rushed by. At first, I resented this swift passage of time. Then I was grateful, because as my mind recalled former Christmases, I was saddened and depressed at the changes in my life.

No more could I spontaneously run out in the snow or sing carols for the neighbors; these and other pleasures were gone forever, and everyone seemed to sense it. There were no tears, at least not now, but the air of sadness was awful.

It wasn't until I was back in my bed at Greenoaks that I allowed myself to cry. Then there was no stopping. B.J., Betty, Denise, and Ann had also gone home for a one-day Christmas visit. But for those who went and for those who had nowhere to go, Christmas was the same: a sad, depressing reminder of better times and happier places when we had been whole.

I tried to evaluate my feelings about what had happened at Christmas. I was happy and thrilled about going home; but, I was sobered by the experience of having to relate to familiar people and old surroundings in strange, new ways.

When the nurse came by the next day, she examined me and said, "Joni, I'm sorry, but that will have to be your last visit home for quite awhile."

"Why?"

"Because it opened all the sores on your back and hips! Your bone protrusions are rubbing the skin away. They won't heal at all unless we put you back in the Stryker Frame," she said simply.

"But can't I sit up at all?" I begged.

"I'm sorry, no. Sitting up is what stretches the skin of the wounds and breaks open the sores. Let's wait until they heal."

Dick came by as often as he could, hitchhiking the sixty-mile round trip from the University of Maryland. I could tell that my accident was really taking a toll on him; his emotions were as frayed as mine.

"Dickie," I told him one day, "we're holding onto the past. We can't do that. We can't go back to high school times."

He looked at me sadly and nodded. "But things will get better. Soon you'll be — "

"No!" I cried. "They won't get better. Don't you understand? I'm not going to get better! Don't you see that?"

Once again, I desperately wanted to kill myself.

Here I was, trapped in this canvas cocoon. I couldn't move anything except my head. Physically, I was little more than a corpse. I had no hope of ever walking again. I could never lead a normal life and marry Dick. *In fact, he might even be walking out of my life forever*, I concluded. I had absolutely no idea of how I could find purpose or meaning in just existing day after day — waking, eating, watching TV, sleeping.

Why on earth should a person be forced to live out such a dreary existence? How I prayed for some accident or miracle to kill me. The mental and spiritual anguish was as unbearable as the physical torture.

But once again, there was no way for me to commit suicide. This frustration was also unbearable. I was despondent, but I was also angry because of my helplessness. How I wished for strength and control enough in my fingers to do something, anything, *to end my life*. Tears of rage, fear, and frustration only added to my despondency.

There was an added complication to my lack of well-being. The sores, caused by my protruding bones, did not heal. In fact, the doctors insisted surgery was the only way to correct the problem. So, on June 1, 1968, I was driven back to City Hospital for bone operations, further confirmation that my injury was permanent. The doctors would not shave the bony protuberances from my hip and tailbone if there was any hope of my using my legs again.

The surgeon, Dr. Southfield, explained the operation.

"Since you have no feeling, it will not be necessary to anesthetize you. But if you're squeamish about the sight of blood and tissue — ."

"Never mind," I said curtly. "I've been through it all. I've been here almost a year, remember. There isn't much I haven't seen. And there's precious little they haven't already done to me. Carve away!"

I listened as Dr. Southfield's hands guided the scalpel through the flesh on my hip. Blood spurted behind the blade as he laid back the skin and muscle tissue. Assistants gave him various surgical tools as he called for them.

In a few minutes, I could hear a strange rasping, scraping sound as he chiseled away on my hip bone, filing down the sharp, jutting joints that caused my bed sores.

In spite of my earlier bluster, I didn't like the sights and sounds of the surgery. I felt queasy, so I began to sing, taking my mind off the operation. I sang loud and long, going through a terribly depressing assortment of pessimistic songs.

"Can't you sing something else — something brighter?" asked Dr. Southfield.

"No!" I snapped and kept up my "concert."

After awhile, I was turned over, and the surgeon began to operate on my tailbone. He shaved and chiseled more bony protuberances. Finally, he sutured all the incisions. Then I was bandaged, examined, and driven back to Greenoaks for recuperation.

When the sutures and bedsores healed, I was allowed to sit up slowly. Earl carefully placed me in bed and tried to help me sit up.

"Here we go, Joni," he said. "Take it nice and slow. Don't want 'cha to get dizzy and pass out. Right?"

"Right," I echoed.

"Easy now."

"How'm I doing, Earl? I'm sitting up! How about that!"

Earl did not reply. Soon he quietly carried me back to the Stryker Frame.

"Hey. Leave me in bed, Earl," I commanded. "I've waited to sit up again. If you're worried about me passing out — ."

"Sorry, Joni. I gotta put you back. The operation didn't take. Your backbone just busted the incision open again. You're bleeding."

*   *   *   *

As I lay in the Stryker through the following long weeks, I finally gave up ever hoping to walk. But I began to strain every atom of will power into getting back the use of my hands. If I had my hands, I wouldn't be so helpless. I wouldn't have to depend on Jay or Diana to wash or brush my hair. Or put on make-up. Or just feed myself. If I could only do something — anything at all — I wouldn't feel so helpless.

"You can use your mouth to do some of the things you'd normally do with hands," suggested therapist Chris Brown one day after learning of my feelings. She added, "You've seen people in O.T. (occupational therapy) learn to write or type by holding a pencil or stick with their teeth. You can learn, too."

"No," I said. "It's disgusting. Degrading. I won't do it!"

Chris did not press me. "Maybe some other day," she said.

Later, Jay came to see me. Although she smiled and seemed in control, she'd been crying again.

"Hi, sis," she said.

"You've been crying, Jay."

Jay nodded. She never wanted to worry me with her own problems and often hid her feelings from me, but I had eventually learned of the difficulties she was having with her marriage. Now her divorce had become final.

She said evenly, "It's over. And it'll be all right, Joni. Don't worry."

"But — "

"Really. Don't worry." Jay changed the subject. "Here, I've brought you some goodies." She opened a bag of doughnuts and held one up. "Your favorites, see?"

We spent an hour or so chatting and reading through a *Seventeen* magazine she spread out beneath the frame.

Then, as she prepared to leave, she looked soberly into my eyes and said, "Joni, I want — I want you to come and live with little Kay and me when you get out of the hospital."

"Let's think about it, Jay," I replied. "We'll see, okay?"

She kissed me on the cheek and ran the back of her hand across my forehead. Smiling, she left.

The significance of Jay's visit slowly sank into my consciousness, and I pondered her comments and offer. I promised myself not to make any plans, although the thought of living with Jay was reassuring.

When Dick came by later, he wheeled my Stryker to the game room and sat on the floor under me so we could talk. We were trying out a new relationship — being friends only. While neither of us had really discussed such a change, we each had assumed that we had no immediate future together as husband and wife. First, I'd have to get my hands back. Then I'd have to be rehabilitated, and that would probably take a long time. So neither of us talked about things like love and marriage.

His visits consisted mostly of friendly encouragement — and reading to me, usually from a modern New Testament translation. The message was there, loud and clear: faith, hope, trust. But I dismissed this as being too superficial. Fine for the ordinary person on his feet dealing with life, temptation, and doubt. But what was God saying to me, encased immobile in my Stryker?

Diana read to me from the Old Testament, and I began to identify with many of the prophets. Like Jeremiah, I thought perhaps God's wrath was being poured out on me in judgment.

I read the poetry of the Book of Lamentations and identified fully with the sorrows about which Jeremiah had written:

"She weeps bitterly at night,
    the tears flow always on her cheeks;
no one of all her lovers
    now seeks to bring her comfort."

> *Oh, God, how*
> *true. And I can't*
> *even wipe my own*
> *tears away!*

"For the Lord has afflicted her
    because of the greatness of her
    transgressions."

Yes! I broke His moral
commandments.
Now punishment.

"Look and see if there is any sorrow
    like my sorrow,
  which is being dealt out to me,
which the Lord has inflicted
    in the day of His fiery anger.

No one else is being
punished like this. Why
did God do this to me?

"From on high He sent fire into my
    bones,
  and it has subdued them."

Diving accident . . .
paralysis . . .

"He has given me over to frustration
  and faintness all day long."

rage . . .
weakness and fear.

"He has made my strength to fail.
The Lord has delivered me into hands
  which I am unable to withstand."

In bed for a year,
completely dependent
on orderlies and nurses.

"My eyes are exhausted with weeping;
    my emotions are deeply disturbed;
  my grief is poured out on the earth."

How much more can
I take? I'm at the
end of my rope!

"Surely He has turned away from me;

He has turned His hand against me
    all the day."
                Why, God . . .
                why?
                why?
"He has made my skin and my flesh
    turn old:
He has crushed my bones."
                The bedsores, stitches,
                bone surgery . . .
"He has piled up against me, and
    surrounded me
with bitterness and distress."
                and I'm still
                surrounded by canvas,
                catheter tubes,
                and urine bags.
"He has caused me to dwell in dark
    places,
as the dead of former times."
                I'm trapped in this
                gloomy hospital where
                we sit like zombies
                waiting to die.
"He has built a wall around me, I
    cannot go forth;
He has weighted me down with
    chains."
                I'm trapped!
                Stryker, straps,
                and Crutchfield tongs . . .
"Even when I cry aloud and call for
    help,
He shuts out my prayer."
                and God doesn't care.
"I have forgotten what enjoyment is."
                He doesn't even care.

(Jeremiah 1:2,5,12-14; 2:11; 3:3-8,17, Berkeley)

*   *   *   *

Who, or What, is God? *Certainly not a personal Being who cares for individuals*, I reasoned. *What's the use of believing when your prayers fall on deaf ears?*

My doubts began to be as deep-seated as my resentment. When Diana or Dick read a promise from the Bible concerning hope or trust, I shut them off.

"That's too pat," I told them. "Those verses are too glib to have anything but surface meaning. Try to apply those promises to me. You tell me how my being here for over a year 'works together for good.' What good? Where? When? I don't want to hear any more!"

And there were people at Greenoaks who added to my feelings of helplessness and depression. Mrs. Barber, attendant on the midnight shift, was as angry and bitter as I was for reasons of her own. She'd often make obscene or insensitive comments designed to hurt and demean those of us who got in her way. To Mrs. Barber, we were not patients in need of care, but hindrances to her routine of chores which had to be done.

One night, she came into our room and angrily swept my pictures off the window air conditioner near my Stryker. "How the —— do you think I can turn on this —— air conditioner with all this —— on it?" she hissed. The pictures had been there for weeks and in no way interfered with its operation.

She picked out a photo of Dick and said terrible things — including that Dick was involved in all kinds of lewd and vulgar conduct. Her perversity sickened me, and I snapped back at her.

She came over to my Stryker and snarled, "I ought to leave you like this until morning and not flip you. But to show you what a nice person I am, I'll turn you." With that, she flipped me violently. She had not taken the usual precaution of checking to see that my arms were tucked in first. One arm was loose, and when she spun me, my hand struck violently against the Stryker.

Although my hand was paralyzed and I could feel no pain, it began to swell and was badly bruised. She left the injured arm dangling and rushed out of the room to other duties.

Shaken, angry and afraid, I began to sob quietly.

"I saw what she did, Joni," said B.J. "You ought to report her to the supervisor."

"Yeah. I heard everything. You oughtta turn her in," added Denise.

"But I can't report her. She'll do something else — worse," I sobbed.

The next day, however, mom came to visit and asked about my swollen and bruised hand. I tried to dismiss it lightly as an accident, but the girls told mom what had happened. Incensed, mom went directly to the supervisor and complained in the most vocal terms.

Late that night, Mrs. Barber came into our darkened room, approached me quietly, and put her face next to mine. With a voice that was both whisper and evil menace, she said, "If you ever say anything against me again, you ——, I'll see that you pay for it dearly! Do you understand, you ——?"

It was no idle threat. I was terrified, frightened that something horrible would happen to me if I did complain.

In addition to the few who were like Mrs. Barber, who hated patients and having to care for them, there were others who did care, but only a few had time. Nurses seemed to have time only to fill out medication and defecation charts. Most attendants were overworked and poorly paid, and — as a result — some just didn't care.

These episodes only added to my depression. Jim Pollard was a bright, young quadriplegic who was asking many of the same questions I was. His muscles wouldn't quite support his head, so it dropped slightly to the left. But his voice, mind, and spirit were strong.

"If there isn't a personal God who cares about me, then what's the use?" I asked him.

"That's the whole point," he explained. "I've done a lot of reading and studying. I've looked at religion, philosophy, everything. Life has absolutely no meaning. It's pointless. Absurd."

"Then why bother?" I countered. "Why not just

commit suicide? In fact, why doesn't the whole human race commit suicide if life has no meaning?"

"Oh, it can have meaning. Some people believe in God, and that gives them meaning. But when the chips are down — like for us here — you see just how shallow religion is," he said earnestly.

"But do you think life makes sense?"

"Probably not for us. People on their feet can eat, work, and make love — all kinds of things. 'Pursuit of happiness' and all that, y'know?"

I nodded.

"But here. Well, that's a different story. We've reduced life to its barest elements. And, for the most part, there's no reason to live."

"Then why are you still alive?"

Jim shrugged. "Guess I'm just not gutsy enough to do myself in. Besides, life does have meaning if you find it for yourself."

"How?"

"Your mind. Intelligence. I get a kick out of developing my mind. To h _ _ _ with my body. Maybe I can find something in being intelligent."

"Maybe," I offered. "But what about everyone else? Everyone on their feet. They're born. They live and die with existence as their only goal. Why bother?"

"You've got me, Joni," he answered. "Why not read some of my books and tracts. I've got some stuff here by Sartre, Marx, and other great minds."

I read it all, and it all pointed me further and further from God and hope — the meaning of life was that *it had no meaning*. Life without an eternal focus, without God, led to despair. I could see this but didn't know what else to believe. Had not God, if there was a God, turned His back on me?

Jim continued to counsel me in agnosticism. "You see, Joni, nothing will ever make sense. Accept it. Life is capricious as well as temporal. Jobs, success, friends, family — these only have meaning as a means to that end. You're only here for the moment, so if you want anything out of life, get it now. Don't get the idea you're putting something away for an afterlife."

"But the trouble is, Jim," I interrupted, "I found out in high school that temporal things don't satisfy me. There has to be something permanent."

"What about your accident? That sure isn't temporary," he reminded me. "You've told me the Bible says even your paralysis works out for good. How? What's the purpose of your paralysis?"

"I — I don't know. That's what's making me doubt God. If He was real, wouldn't He show me? Wouldn't I have some sense of purpose with it all?"

Jim said, "You're just outgrowing your need for religion and God, Joni. Did you read any of the other books I gave you?"

"Yes. I read *Siddhartha* and Kafka's *The Trial, Bio-Ethics* — uh — *Man's Search for Meaning*. All of them. I've read every existentialist author you've given me," I told him.

"Well, I'm impressed. Then you ought to know by now that the idea of a personal God is ridiculous."

"I'm not there yet, Jim. I don't know. I've read everything you've given me. These books. build a pretty strong case for your point of view. But — "

"But you're afraid. You think God is sitting up there in heaven waiting to zap you if you have doubts. Well, tell me, Joni. If there is a God, what can He do to you that hasn't been done already? That's the way I look at it. I'm crippled. For good. I'll never be on my feet again. What's God going to do if I don't believe? Damn me to hell? I'm already in hell! No — there's no God, Joni. No God — " His voice trailed off wistfully, as though he had once held out hope that somehow God did exist. Yet now, convinced in his unbelief, Jim was resigned. "There's no God."

I prayed desperately: "God I have just two choices: either You exist or You don't. If You don't exist, then I don't see any logical reason for living. If people who believe are only going through motions that mean nothing, I want to know. Why should we go on fooling ourselves? Life is absurd most of the time. And it seems man's only end is despair. What can I do, Lord? I want to believe, but I have nothing to hang on to. God, You've got to prove Your existence to me!"

My mind was a jumble of thoughts and philosophies. Logical, rational, intellectual positions were posed and just as quickly disposed of by opposing concepts, apparently just as valid. What was right? What was wrong? Truth? Oh, what a maze of confusion. *Am I losing my mind as well as my body?*

Weary from thinking, my eyelids fell shut. Then, from somewhere, a calmness took over. A thought — or memory — "a still, small voice" — reminded my troubled brain, *Thou wilt keep him in perfect peace whose mind is stayed on thee.*

And I slept.

Six

Diana came by more and more now. She came so often, in fact, that some visitors thought she was one of the staff. One day she put down the Bible she'd been reading from and said, "Joni, I've decided to be a volunteer worker here so I can take better care of you."

"But, Diana, you can't drop out of school," I protested.

"I've prayed about it a lot, Joni. I believe it's what God wants me to do. You see, I don't know what the Lord has planned for me in the future. I'm going to drop out for a semester or so and ask God for specific guidance for the future," she explained.

"Yes, but — "

Diana interrupted, "But nothing. While I'm seeking God's will on this, I'll be a volunteer — at least until next fall."

"Diana, I appreciate what you want to do. But are you sure it's the right thing?" I asked.

She nodded. Her eyes were bright with determination. "Yes. I've made up my mind, and I have real peace about it."

It was good to have Diana around as a hospital volunteer. She busied herself with other patients as well as me. And she watched the nurses and therapists so she could help in even more areas.

Meanwhile, my spiritual confusion was leading me down blind alleys. In my attempts to be open-minded about other concepts, as opposed to belief in God, I became even more confused and frustrated. The more I read, the more tangled my beliefs became. Was there no such thing as truth and meaning? All my reading of Sartre, Hesse, Marx, and others brought me no light.

It seemed the further I opened my mind to these philosophies which denied God, the further I went away from Him. Finally, I became convinced there was little to be learned or understood from these confusing writings. My search had led me back to the Bible.

I began to sense that God was real and that He was dealing with me.

"My thoughts are not your thoughts. My ways are not your ways," He reminded me from His Word. I needed to understand that — that I could not comprehend my own purpose or meaning without taking God's deity into consideration.

"What do you mean?" asked Diana when we were discussing this subject one day.

"Well, I've been trying to have the world make sense by having things to relate to me. I want to see my life have meaning and purpose. But the Bible says our purpose is to glorify God. My life has meaning when I glorify God," I explained.

"Yes, I understand," said Diana. "But how do you get that concept to work?"

"I'm not sure. But I know until now I've been looking for a way to make the world revolve around me. Now I'm convinced that I need to plug in some other way."

"Well, the answers to all questions are in the Bible," offered Diana. "Maybe if you look for them, you'll find God's will."

"Yeah," I replied. "I think I get impatient because I

don't see life as God does. A year in a Stryker seems like
a century to me — but a year isn't much time to God. His
frame of reference is eternity. Maybe things just take a
little longer than I expect."

"What's next then, Joni?"

"I don't know. I — I guess I'll have to take things
one at a time. One, I'm paralyzed and don't know why
God allowed it to happen to me. But maybe I'll never
know why. Maybe I shouldn't let it hang me up."

"Then concentrate on getting out of here," urged
Diana.

"Yeah, well, I suppose so. I'm scared, Di. I'm
scared, I guess, because I don't know what'll happen
when I do go home."

"But that's the whole point of trusting the Lord,
Joni." She was smiling, her eyes wide in the enjoyment of
a new truth which had just come to her. "You don't have
to know why God let you be hurt. The fact is, God knows
— and that's all that counts. Just trust Him to work things
out for good, eventually, if not right now."

"What do you mean?"

"Would you be any happier if you did know why
God wants you paralyzed? I doubt it. So don't get worked
up about trying to find meaning to the accident," she
scolded.

"Then what do you think I should do?"

"Well, therapy, for one thing. You know how you've
avoided occupational therapy — you've said 'what's the
use of learning to write with a stick in my mouth?' Well, if
God knows the ultimate purpose and meaning of things,
then He can find or give meaning to a paralyzed life, too.
But you can't fight Him on it."

"But I'm making progress in physical therapy. Why
should I learn how to write with my mouth? I expect to get
the use of my hands back!"

"But," Diana paused carefully, "but what if you
don't get your hands back?"

I didn't answer right away. The possibility was not
even an option as far as I was concerned. I thought, *I can
give up a year or more of my life to lie here paralyzed. I can*

*even sacrifice my legs and spend the rest of my life in a
wheelchair. I won't complain. But, God, You wouldn't
keep me from getting my hands back and leading a fairly
normal life! You wouldn't leave me like this forever, would
You?*

"Joni — "

"Yes."

"Maybe we shouldn't think about the future just
now," said Diana softly, as if reading my mind. "Let's
just take it one step at a time, like you said."

"I guess I haven't been setting my mind toward
getting out of here. After all, this is a rehab hospital. I
should be concentrating on being rehabilitated, huh?"

The next day, I told Chris Brown, my occupational
therapist, that I wanted to learn how to do things using my
mouth.

Chris was every bit as pleasant, cheerful, helpful,
and encouraging as Joe and Earl, my two physical
therapy aides.

"My job," she explained simply, "is to help you
learn how to function out there, in the world."

"That's all, huh?" I kidded.

"Well, you'll be doing all the work. So my job is
easy."

"What are you going to teach me?"

"Well, first, how about learning how to write?"

"Okay, Chris, what do I do?" I asked.

"Hold this pencil in your mouth. Grip it with your
teeth, like this," Chris explained. She held a pencil in
her own mouth to demonstrate and placed one in my
mouth.

"Okay. Good. See, it's easy. Uh — not so tight.
Don't clench it in your teeth, or you'll get writer's cramp
in your jaw," she joked. "Just hold it firmly so you won't
drop it — tight enough to control it. See?"

"Mm-mff," I mumbled, meaning I understood.

Chris taught me how to make lines, circles, and
other marks. At first these were squiggly and wobbly. But
after many hours of practice, I began to have more
control.

Finally, I was able to make letters. With determination and concentration, I wrote a letter to mom and dad. It was brief, and the letters were still big, awkward squiggles, but it was writing!

This sense of accomplishment gave me a more positive attitude, and I began to enjoy my therapy, reinforced by the encouragement of a staff and patients who cheered every fragment of progress.

In September, I was taken to Kernans Hospital for a second back operation. I didn't really want to go, but my protruding backbone was still making it impossible for bedsores on my back and bottom to heal. This hospital was only a mile away from our house in Woodlawn, so it was difficult for me to deal with the emotions of being so close to home, yet knowing I couldn't return there.

This time, the operation was successful, for which I thanked God. However, I still faced fifteen days of lying face down in my Stryker. During this time of recuperation, I had a bout with the flu and did a lot of reading. To balance all the negative, agnostic, and atheistic books I had read earlier, I now turned to the Bible and helpful Christian literature.

Mom patiently held the books for me for hours as I read. *Mere Christianity* by C. S. Lewis was a refreshing change and gave a beautiful balance to all that I'd been reading before. It helped my spiritual outlook tremendously.

On October 15, my birthday, I received a most welcome and appreciated gift — I was finally turned face up! It was a grand occasion. Diana, mom and dad, Jay, and Dick all visited me. While there had been a transition in our relationship from sweethearts to intimate friends, Dick was just as faithful as ever in coming to see me.

Back at Greenoaks, things began to look brighter for me. Because the operation was a success, I would eventually begin to use a wheelchair, and I was having an easier time in my various forms of therapy.

It was also encouraging to see people leaving Greenoaks. Some of my paraplegic friends had been rehabilitated and were free to go home and find their way back into the world. This seemed exciting to me — so much so that I plunged into my own rehab with renewed determination.

Chris Brown was eager to tap this new energy and enthusiasm. "Why not do something artistic now, since you can write pretty well using your mouth?"

"Artistic?" I asked.

"Yes. You've shown me drawings you did in the past. You enjoy creative things. You can paint these ceramic discs. They make nice gifts," she explained.

I watched as another quadriplegic held a paint brush in her mouth and slopped paint on one of the clay pieces. It seemed useless — like a kindergarten game.

"I don't know — " I said quietly.

"Oh, come on, try it," Chris urged.

"All right."

I tried the painting, spilling globs of color and splashing clumsy designs on the clay discs. It was discouraging and frustrating. At first, I hated every minute of it. But when the discs came out of the kiln, they looked half-way acceptable. And as I practiced — as with writing — I improved.

After a few weeks, I had created several Christmas gifts for my family and friends. I didn't know what they'd think of the nut or candy dishes, but I thought they were pretty good — considering. And it gave me satisfaction to know that I had done them myself.

One day, Chris brought me some moist clay.

"What's that for?" I asked.

"I want you to draw a picture on it."

"How? With a pencil in my mouth?"

"Try this stylus."

"What should I make? Should I write something?"

"Why not do something to express yourself? Make something that you like," she suggested.

Carefully I gauged the distance from my mouth to the soft clay, tested the consistency of it with the pointed stick, then tried to etch something.

I told Chris, "The last time I drew something was on

our trip out West before my accident. All during my childhood daddy encouraged me to draw. He's a self-taught artist." I also recalled that I had particularly enjoyed making charcoal sketches of scenes. Out West, I had filled my sketch pad with drawings of mountains, horses, people, and animals.

I remembered these scenes now and tried to re-member the unconscious process of drawing — how the mental image was communicated to my hands, which moved to transfer the scene to paper. My hands held the key to my talent as an artist. Or did they?

I looked down at the simple sketch I had just done. It was a line drawing of a cowboy and horse etched in the soft clay. It wasn't terribly creative or impressive, but it was a beginning.

Chris seemed amazed at my first attempt. "Joni, that's great! You've got real talent." She grinned and said, "You should have done this before. You need to get back to your art."

"But that was when I had hands," I protested.

She shook her head. "Doesn't matter. Hands are tools. That's all. The skill, the talent, is in the brain. Once you've practiced, you can do as well with your mouth as you did with your hands!"

"Wow — really?" I asked.

"Yeah! Want to try?"

"Sure! Let's do it."

It was an enormously satisfying day for me. For the first time in almost a year and a half, I was able to express myself in a productive, creative way. It was exciting and gave me renewed hope.

My spiritual temperature was improving, too. Ear-lier, my anger and confusion had turned to resentment. I thought, *How can a loving God – if such exists – allow this desperate situation?* My search into other areas didn't turn up a reasonable answer, so when I turned back to the Bible, my bitterness was softened.

I was angry that my life had been reduced to the basics of eating, breathing, and sleeping — day in and day out. But what I discovered was that the rest of the human race was in the same boat. Their lives revolved around the same meaningless cycle — except with them, it wasn't as obvious. Peripheral things distracted them from the fact that they were caught on the same treadmill. Their jobs, school, families, and recreation occupied them enough so they never consciously recognized that their lives were the same as mine — eating, breathing, sleeping.

And slowly I became aware of God's interest in me. I was some sort of "cosmic guinea pig" — a representative of the human race on whom truth could be tested. All the distractions, trappings, and things were gone. God had taken them away and had placed me here without distractions. My life was reduced to absolute basics. So now what? *What am I to do with my life?* I wondered. *I have no body, but I am still someone.* I had to find meaning, purpose, and direction, not just some measure of temporary satisfaction.

Even the clean, sterile sheets in the austere ward were symbolic. Eating, breathing, sleeping. Eating, breathing, sleeping. *For what purpose? How can I glorify God? What can I do?*

Yes, there has to be a personal God, I reasoned. He may choose not to reveal Himself to me in some spectacular way — but then, why should He? Why was I any more important than the next person who had to find God and purpose by faith, not sight? Why should I be different?

I told Diana of my thoughts. "Nothing is really making any sense yet, Diana. I don't know what God is doing — but I believe He is real and that somehow He knows — and understands. There's a positive aspect to my thoughts now. I'm still confused, but before, my confusion leaned toward doubt. Now it leans toward trust."

"Maybe it has something to do with your prayer before the accident," Diana suggested.

"What prayer?"

"Remember? You told me that shortly before your accident, you prayed, 'Lord, do something in my life to

change me and turn me around.' Maybe this is God's way
of answering that prayer."

"I've wondered about that myself. It could be. But
it's sure not what I expected. And He certainly has His
own timetable!" I said, adding, "I don't know His purpose in this. I probably won't ever walk again. And I
don't see how I can ever be happy again. I guess that's
what really bothers me."

"Not being happy?"

"Yeah. I mean, if there's one thing I learned from
those existentialist writers, it's 'man cannot live with
despair.' Do you think I can ever be happy, Diana?"

"I don't know, Joni — I don't know."

My studies in the Scriptures began in earnest now,
along with other Christian literature. Writings by Francis
Schaeffer and C. S. Lewis seemed like a breath of fresh
air compared with Marx, Hesse, and the non-Christian
books I'd read. I began to sense a direct application of
and appreciation for the Word of God in my life. For the
first time, I saw meaning for me in the Bible. My own
"fiery trials" were now a little easier to cope with as I saw
how I fit in with God's scheme of things, especially
through reading the Psalms. "The Lord will sustain him
(me) upon his (my) sickbed" (Ps. 41:3 NAS).

Pressures seemed greatest at night. Perhaps therapy had gone badly that day. Or no one came to visit. Or
maybe Mrs. Barber was being mean to me again. Whatever the problem, I'd want to cry. I felt even more
frustrated because I couldn't cry, for there was no one to
wipe my eyes and help me blow my nose. The Scriptures
were encouraging, and I'd apply the reality and truth of
them to my own special needs. During these difficult
midnight hours, I'd visualize Jesus standing beside my
Stryker. I imagined Him as a strong, comforting person
with a deep, reassuring voice, saying specifically to me,
"Lo, I am with you always. If I loved you enough to die for
you, don't you think I ought to know best how to run your
life even if it means your being paralyzed?" The reality of
this Scripture was that He was with me, now. Beside me
in my own room! That was the comfort I needed.

I discovered that the Lord Jesus Christ could indeed empathize with my situation. On the cross for those agonizing, horrible hours, waiting for death, He was immobilized, helpless, paralyzed.

Jesus did know what it was like not to be able to move — not to be able to scratch your nose, shift your weight, wipe your eyes. *He was paralyzed on the cross.* He could not move His arms or legs. Christ knew exactly how I felt! "Therefore, since we have a great high priest who has gone into heaven, Jesus the Son of God, let us hold firmly to the faith we profess. For we do not have a high priest who is unable to sympathize with our weaknesses, but we have one who has been tempted in every way, just as we are" (Heb. 4:14, 15, NIV).

Before my accident, I didn't "need" Christ. Now I needed Him desperately. When I had been on my feet, it never seemed important that He be part of my decision-making — what party to go to, whether to go to a friend's house or a football game, etc. It didn't seem that He would even be interested in such insignificant things. But, now that my life was reduced to the basic life-routines, He was a part of it because He cared for me. He was, in fact, my only dependable reality.

These new and reassuring concepts had a quieting effect on my spirit, and I think they were even helpful as I shared them with Jay during her personal troubles.

My drawing, still self-expression in style and simple in approach, was more of a therapy than I had anticipated. As a reflection of my new mood, I began to sign "PTL" on my drawings — for "praise the Lord" — an expression of my belief that God cared for me. It was a simple expression, giving Him the glory for His direct help in restoring this one aspect of my individuality.

I also began to take more of an interest in my personal grooming. Before, I had avoided all mirrors. Now, Jay and Diana helped me fix my hair, brighten my face, find and wear attractive clothes, and discover ways to improve my overall appearance.

In therapy, I was able to try sitting up. I was

bothered by dizziness and nausea again as they lifted me to a sitting position in my new bed, with my legs dangling over the edge. It was a slow process, but soon I was almost upright. Then I used the slant-board to get used to the vertical position again, while muscles, long unused, had to get accustomed to holding up my head. When my inner ear and neck muscles adjusted to the vertical once more, I was allowed to sit in a wheelchair. My legs were wrapped in elastic bandages to avoid circulation problems caused by blood settling in the arteries of my legs and thighs, and I was fitted with a tight corset that supported my upper torso. This enabled me to sit up and breathe comfortably.

I was excited about my progress and looked forward to going home for the Christmas holidays again. Christmas, 1968 — a whole year had passed since I was last home! But this time I could go home for several days.

Just before Christmas, dad and mom brought me some interesting news.

"Joni, we've heard about a new hospital in California," said dad. "It's called Rancho Los Amigos, it's in Los Angeles, and they are making some pretty remarkable advancements in therapy."

"Their approach to rehabilitation is very progressive," mom added. "They've been able to teach people to regain the use of their arms and legs. Even so-called impossible cases."

"Oh, wow!" I exclaimed. "Yeah! Let's go there. Can we?"

"We're checking now. We expect to hear soon. But I think it looks good," said dad. "We can't go with you, but we've talked with Jay, and she wants to go. She could fly out and rent an apartment nearby to be with you."

"That sounds marvelous!" I shrieked. "Let's pray that God will make it possible. Wow — wouldn't that be some Christmas present?"

It was an exciting Christmas. I was strong enough to stay at home for several days, and it was good to be in normal surroundings once more. And when Dick asked me to go with him to a movie, I was really thrilled.

But as much as I dearly wanted to be normal again, it was impossible. Dick put his arm around me, and I didn't even know it. He squeezed me affectionately, lovingly — but I couldn't feel a thing. I kept watching the movie. Finally he asked, "Don't you feel that?"

"What?"

"This." He squeezed me again.

"No," I said softly, embarrassed. "I — I'm sorry." I really wanted to feel his arm, his touch.

Driving home, Dick was forced to stop the car suddenly, and I flew forward and hit my head on the dash. I couldn't help myself — couldn't even pick myself up. I was not hurt. Only my pride and ego were damaged.

Dick berated himself for letting this happen. "Why didn't I remember to hold on to you?" he scolded himself.

"Dick, please don't blame yourself. It takes getting used to. And I'm not hurt. Let's not allow it to spoil our evening."

We drove home without further incident. As Dick wheeled me into the house, I said, "Dickie, thank you. Oh, wow, did I have fun! It — it was almost like the exciting things we used to do. This is the first time I've done anything normal in a year and a half. Thank you, Dickie."

"It was a lot of fun," he said simply and leaned across to kiss me on the forehead. "Glad you enjoyed yourself." His ever-sensitive eyes smiled lovingly into mine.

It was fun. But it wasn't really like the "old times." We were both still uncomfortable and awkward with my chair, and I wondered, *Will things ever be normal again?*

I promised myself to do everything I could to make it happen, at least with my attitude. What a contrast with last Christmas! A year before, I had had only a day at home, and I had been so ashamed of my appearance and handicap that I had cringed in the background and covered my legs with the old brown blanket.

This year, I wore new hose and a bright orange sweater with stylishly short corduroy skirt to match. My hair, although still short, was done in a casual, feminine style, and I felt like a woman again, not just a body stuffed in hospital pajamas!

This time I did not want to go back to Greenoaks.

"You won't have to, Joni," said dad.

"What?"

"You won't have to go back to Greenoaks. We've just received word from California. Rancho Los Amigos has room for you. We'll be leaving next week, after New Year's."

I began to cry. "Oh, daddy, I'm so happy. The Lord is real. He does answer prayer."

"Mother and I will fly out there with you, and Jay will drive out and meet us there."

"I can't believe I'm really going."

Rancho Los Amigos — that's where I'll get back my hands, I thought.

Seven

The flight to California was a memorable experience. After all, it was my first flight, and I was flying toward *hope*. I'd soon regain the use of my hands — Dick and I could resume our relationship and get married. At last I could see what I thought was God's pattern "for good" for my life.

When we arrived in Los Angeles — some 3,018 miles from the freezing cold and icy streets of Baltimore — the weather was balmy and sunny. I knew immediately that I was going to enjoy my stay.

Remembering my disappointment at my first sight of Greenoaks, I purposely avoided making a mental picture of Rancho Los Amigos. To my surprise, Rancho was beautiful and well-staffed. Many of the orderlies and staff people were college students working their way through school. Several were girls, and I was glad to have people of my own age and background to whom I could relate.

I was impressed by the order and controlled activity of this place. At Greenoaks, the staff people were always busy, but it was the kind of chaotic busyness of those who are overworked. Here, there was no lost motion. Though everyone had plenty to do, it was for the benefit of the patient, not at his expense. I'm sure that this was due to the fact that Rancho was well-staffed and the people well-paid.

Mom and dad stayed long enough to get me comfortably settled; then they returned to Baltimore, leaving Jay and Kay in a rented apartment near Rancho Los Amigos. One night, about a week later, I heard a commotion in the hall. I strained to hear the voices — there was no mistaking them. Exploding into my room were Diana, Dick, and Jackie!

"Ta da!" sang Diana, gesturing and bowing outlandishly.

"I can't believe it!" I shrieked.

"We got lonesome," grinned Dick.

"Glad to see us?" asked Jackie.

"Oh, you guys! How did you get here?"

"We drove all the way," said Diana.

"Non-stop," added Dick. "That's why we're so grubby."

"Yeah," smiled Jackie, "we came directly to the hospital. We gassed up in Nevada and haven't made any stops since then — we wanted to get here tonight before visiting hours ended."

"I think we drove the last fifty miles on gas fumes," laughed Dick.

"You guys are too much!" I said. It was a wild, exuberant reunion, and a few rules regarding visitors were "bent" that night as they shared the details of their trip with me. They all talked excitedly and at once, alternately flopping on my bed and punctuating their conversation with wild gestures and contagious laughter.

Jay and Kay arrived before they left and promptly invited them to bring their sleeping bags and camp out at the apartment during their visit.

Therapy at Rancho began immediately and consisted of trying to get me to become as independent as possible. I was fitted with braces for my forearms and taught how to use shoulder and back muscles to get my arms to respond. By "throwing" certain muscles, I found that I could raise and lower my arms to some extent, but I could not move my fingers or bend my wrists, limiting the movements and use of my arms, as well as control of these movements. I could not pick up or grasp even the easiest item or utensil.

However, I did learn to feed myself. A spoon was bent at a 45-degree angle and attached to my arm brace. By moving my arm, I could swing it into a plate of food, scoop up a bite, and lift it back toward my mouth. The movement — smooth, easy, and unconscious for seventeen years of my life — was now awkward and difficult and required supreme concentration. By raising and lowering the spoon into the food on the plate, I was able to feed myself. The movement was like that of a steam shovel, and often I spilled more than I got in my mouth. But it was an exciting experience — feeding myself for the first time in a year and a half!

Gradually my movements became smoother, and I tried a fork, bent in the same way, with moderate success. It's a small thing to be able to lift a bite of mashed potatoes to your mouth, but the sense of accomplishment for me was thrilling.

My doctor at Rancho was a bright young specialist whose methods were new and, perhaps, a bit unorthodox.

"Thanks for not sending my friends away when they burst in here, doctor," I said.

"I don't want anyone chasing your friends away," he responded. "In fact, I want them to come — as often as they can."

"Really?"

"Yes. I want them to observe you in all your therapy, to learn as much as possible about you and your handicap."

"You mean you want them to watch me doing P.T. and O.T.?"

"Everything. You see, Joni, I want your friends and family to know your procedures, your needs, and your problems as we know them."

"Why, doctor?"

"To help you become less dependent on a hospital for care," he said.

"You want them to learn how to take care of me?"

"That's right. And I want you to set a realistic goal for yourself regarding getting out of here and going home for good."

"H-home?" I stammered.

"I think you should plan to finish here by April 15," he announced.

"April 15! But that's only three months away. Will I be ready?"

"That's up to you. Are you willing to work toward it?"

"Oh, wow, am I?"

This seemed incredible. I was not used to dealing with my rehabilitation in this way. At Greenoaks, I never knew what was happening, if anything. I was forced to be reactionary in my hopes, so I made no plans at all. I simply took things a day at a time. But now I had something to look forward to, and it was only three months away. My head was swimming with thoughts and dreams of going home for good.

Judy, a Christian college student who worked at Rancho part-time as an attendant, became a friend. Her spiritual maturity seemed much greater than mine, so I often talked with her about the Lord, hoping some of her faith might brush off on me. Judy was attending a Bible college nearby and was delighted to share her new-found knowledge of scriptural truth with me. I felt I was making progress now in every area of my life.

Judy came in early one morning, pushing an empty wheelchair, and said, "You have enough sitting up time to be able to use a wheelchair."

"Really? I can make it go? How?"

"You see these eight rubber knobs on the outside of the wheels?"

I nodded.

"Well, you let your arms hang down beside the wheels and get your hands up against these knobs. See?"

"Yeah — but then what?"

She said, "Remember, we've been working on your shoulder muscles. By throwing your shoulders and biceps into the movement, you can make your arms move against the wheel knob. It'll be slow and tedious until you get the hang of it."

"Okay. When do I start?"

"Now. You can drive to P.T.," said Judy.

"But I don't have P.T. until nine o'clock. It's only seven now," I told her.

Judy just grinned. "Right."

It sure is a slow, tedious process, I thought. I was strapped in to keep me from throwing myself to the floor, and it was a good thing. I tried every exercise I could remember to make back and shoulder muscles substitute for the muscles in my arms. And it took me all of those two hours to coax the wheelchair just the thirty feet or so down the corridor to the P.T. area. By then, I was so exhausted and winded, I had no strength left for P.T. exercises!

However, Judy was waiting there to see my progress and grinned widely at my efforts.

"Beautiful!" she said excitedly.

"Really? Does everyone take this long?"

"The first time," Judy nodded. "A lot of them just give up completely — and a few even fall out of the chair."

I felt proud and exhilarated by the accomplishment — the first time in over a year and a half that I had moved myself through my own efforts.

With practice, I was able to improve my wheelchair ability and speed. There were some minor setbacks, though. A few times I veered into a wall and was stuck for thirty or forty minutes until rescued by someone. Finally, I was given an electric-powered chair to use. What a sense of freedom and adventure this gave me. My chair was controlled electrically by a box which I operated by using my arm brace, and I got so good at it that I practically lived in my chair.

The California community surrounding the hospital

had built its sidewalks to accommodate wheelchairs; even the curbs were gently sloped for easy wheelchair traffic. It gave me a sense of independence and satisfaction to be able to go to the nearby Taco Bell for other patients with less freedom to get around. However, it was still humiliating to have people on the street stare or make comments. It was also humbling to "drive" all the way to the Taco Bell only to be stymied there, unable to get the money out to pay the man for my order. He was accustomed to waiting on handicapped people, however, and handled the situation easily and with good humor. He'd place the order securely on my lap, make change from my purse, and joke about entering me in the Ontario Raceway 500.

I didn't enter the stock car competition at Ontario, but I did do some racing. Rick, another quadriplegic, and I each had electric wheelchairs as well as similar backgrounds in competitive sports, and that could only lead to contests.

"I can make my chair go faster than yours," I bragged one day.

"Oh, yeah? That's what you think. Y'wanna race?"

There was a whirring sound as our chairs raced down the corridor in a "50-yard dash." It was a tie.

"We've got to go farther in order to build up speed," Rick grinned. "Let's race from this corner of the building all the way to the other end of the corridor, around the corner, to the front doors. Okay?"

"You're on!" I said.

Judy and another attendant pretended not to notice our high jinks and walked the other way.

"On your mark!" I called to Rick. "Get set! Go!"

We were off side by side, veering crazily and noisily down the hall.

"Don't crowd me, Eareckson," chuckled Rick. "Get over to your own side of the street!"

As we noisily raced by the rooms, patients inside stared or smiled at our game. First Rick's chair pulled into the lead, then mine, then his again.

Neck and neck, we went into the "far turn" — the

right angle turn down the next corridor. I swung into the corridor without even slowing. As I whipped around the corner, I came face to face with a nurse carrying a tray full of bottles and medicines. She froze. I screamed, "Look out!"

Too late. The tray went flying, crashing on the tile floor, and my chair pinned the nurse, screaming, against the wall. I tried to stop the motor by striking at my control box, but I was clumsy and couldn't shut it off. The wheels were spinning, the nurse was shrieking, and Rick was laughing hysterically.

As punishment for my reckless driving, they took away my driving privileges for a while and confined me to low gear when I took to the road again.

Diana, Dick, and Jackie teased me about that for several days. Their "few days" visit now had stretched into three weeks, but finally, they had to go back East. It was a sad but hopeful good-by. I told them to expect me home soon after April 15.

Before he left with the others, Dick held me tight. "I want you to know that I love you very much. I'll be waiting to see you in April." A great sense of security and reassurance came over me as Dick held me in his arms, and I began to be more optimistic about our future together when we could be more than friends again, when I'd get my hands back. Dick and I still hoped and prayed for nothing else. Perhaps we still had a future together.

*   *   *   *

By April 15, 1969, I had reached my goal in rehabilitation and was told I could go home. But a serious question was still unanswered.

"Doctor, I've been working hard to get my hands back. Now I'm beginning to wonder if I ever will."

"No, Joni. You won't ever get your hands back," he said bluntly. "You might as well stop hoping and get used to the idea."

The words were exactly the opposite of what I wanted to hear — what I'd been praying to hear. I wasn't prepared to accept the fact that I'd always be a quadriplegic. Forever dependent, forever helpless.

It was not terribly surprising news. I suppose I'd always suspected it. Yet, I continually hoped that I'd find some miracle cure at Rancho Los Amigos.

Tearfully, I wrote Dick a letter explaining what the doctor had said.

> For some reason, God has chosen not to answer our prayers. Dickie, I'll never be able to use my hands. That means I'll always be dependent and helpless. I can never be a wife. I know you love me as I love you. Yet, God must have something else in mind for us. Let's continue to be friends, Dickie. But I want you to be free to choose other relationships. Date other girls and look for God to lead you to the right one for you for marriage. I can never be that woman. I'm sorry, Dickie, but I can never ask you to be part of such a hopeless relationship. Let's continue our relationship based on friendship.

I didn't sign it "your Joni" as I had done on my other letters to him. This time, I simply signed it, "Joni."

It wasn't easy for me to end that special relationship with Dick; in fact, I was frightened to end it. I loved him, didn't want to lose him, but knew I couldn't marry him — not now. My paralysis was too great a burden to place on his shoulders. And a commitment without marriage was unfair to him. Heavy waves of grief swept over me when I realized that I would never marry Dick, and I knew I had to quit thinking about past promises which couldn't, or shouldn't, be kept.

I had accepted the fate that I'd never walk again. But I had believed I could still join the ranks of those handicapped persons who drive cars, make meals, work with their hands, and put their arms around someone they love. That I'd be able to drink a glass of water, bathe myself, brush my hair, and put on my own make-up. Little things, to be sure, but things important enough to make the difference between one who is merely handicapped and one who is totally dependent.

Now, ever so slowly, the reality of my injury began to sink in — I was to be a quadriplegic *as long as I lived*.

The house Joni's father built for his wife and family in Baltimore.

Joni's parents, Lindy and John Eareckson.

Joni and her father do acrobatics
at the beach, 1965.

Joni and her father on their trip west,
just prior to the accident, 1967.

Joni and two of her sisters on a recent trip to Toronto. Left to right: Kathy, Joni, Jay.

Joni doing trick riding and show riding, 1966.

Her drawing opposite indicates
her remaining interest in horses.

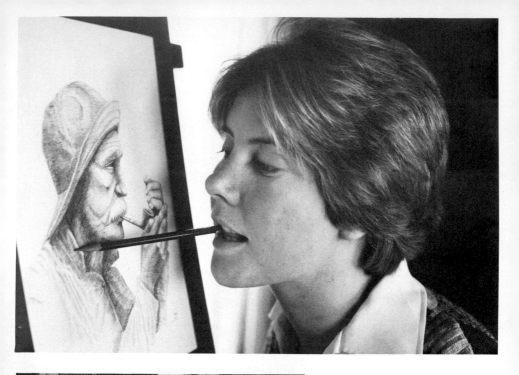

Joni at her easel,
drawing with her mouth.

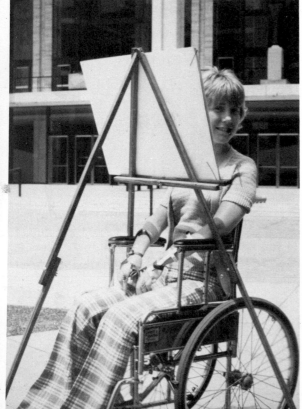

Joni at Lincoln Center Plaza, N.Y.,
exhibiting her artwork, 1975.

 Jay and Joni.

Above: Joni at home.

Dick Filbert, 1971.

Joni in the chair with overhead arm support attachment, aided by neighbors.

Friends gathered for dinner at Joni and Jay's home — the farm in Sykesville.

Diana and Joni in Central Park, N.Y.,1975

Right: Steve Estes, 1975.

Above right and below: Views of the Sykesville farm.

Above left: Joni tells stories to nieces and nephews outside her home.

Opposite page: Diana, Joni, and Jay and outside views of the farm and horses.

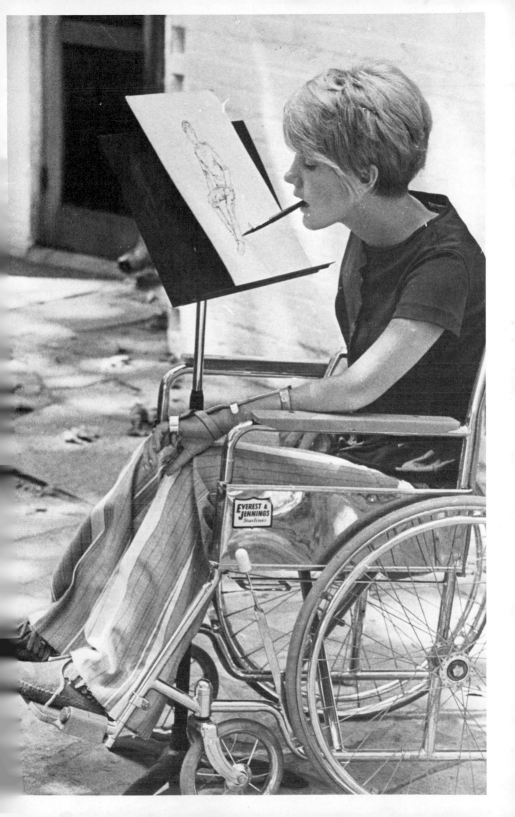

It is important to remember that the promise "...God causes all things to work together for good..." only applies to those who love God, those who have been born into His family. However, due to our sin and rebellion we are alienated from God and subject to His judgment. Praise God though, that He sent His Son, Jesus to be judged on the cross — paying the death penalty for my sin and your sin! If we truly trust that our punishment was borne by Christ and obey Him as our Lord, we can be assured of eternal life and the promise of Romans 8:28.

It is my hope that in the course of reading this book, the Holy Spirit has enlightened your heart and mind to these truths. Jesus is alive and His power is available to you...He proves Himself daily in my life, and what more couldn't He do in your life! Are you a part of God's heavenly family? For indeed, I hope one day we shall meet in glory

Joni
PTL

Eight

When I returned from California, I stoically and glibly thanked God for whatever purpose He had in the fact that I wouldn't get the use of my hands back, that I couldn't ever marry Dick. But I was becoming cynical again and doubting the reality of Romans 8:28.

Mom and dad were glad to have me at home, and I was happy to be there. But inwardly I was bitter and resentful that God had not answered my prayers, had not given me my hands back.

Diana spent a lot of time at our house, taking care of my needs and trying to keep me encouraged.

"I know they told you at Rancho Los Amigos that you'd never be able to walk or use your hands again, but you can't give up," she urged.

"Why not?" I replied dully.

"You've got to work with what you have left."

"I have nothing left."

"Don't give me that," scolded Diana. "I saw people at Greenoaks and Rancho who were really bad off — blind, mute, deaf. Some even lost their minds — they were almost vegetables. *They* have nothing left, Joni. But you have your mind, your voice, your eyes, and your ears. You have everything you need. And you're going to make them work for you if I have anything to say!" she said.

"We'll see — we'll see," I told her.

Dick came to visit, and our conversations seemed awkward and strained. He had never really replied to my letter directly — he never said, "Yeah, Joni, you're right. We can never get married because I can't handle the problems and emotions involved with your handicap."

Finally, one night, he broached the subject. "Joni, I don't care if you get healed or not. If you aren't healed and I'm fortunate enough to marry you, I'll be the only person in the world to whom God gave the gift of a woman in a chair for a wife."

"How can you say such a thing? The gift?"

"Sure. I look at you and your handicap as a special blessing."

"A blessing?!" I interrupted.

"Yes, blessing — because God gives only good gifts," Dick replied simply.

"No, Dickie. It'd never work. My paralysis — that's a lot to handle. It's almost too much for me, let alone you."

"But sharing the burden would make it lighter for each of us."

"That's romantic, but unrealistic," I told him.

Dick was silent. He did not want to accept what I was saying. He was envisioning what he wanted the outcome to be, not what would be. Finally, his eyes ready to spill tears, he smiled and nodded. "You're right, I guess. Maybe — I can't deal with it. Maybe — I'm not up to it — " His voice trailed off.

Eventually Dick did start dating again. But often he'd bring his new girl friends over to the house to meet me. In fact, some of his dates consisted of nothing more than trips to visit me.

*   *   *   *

I withdrew into myself and the solitude of home. After being away so long, I appreciated the old house with all its pleasant memories. Yet for some reason, I couldn't really feel at home there any more; I felt awkward in my own home.

This left me with eerie, anxious feelings — like the depression I felt trying to adjust during those nightmarish months after my accident.

"What's the matter, honey?" dad finally asked.

"I — I don't know, daddy. I'm just sad — depressed."

Dad nodded.

"I don't know if I can ever really adjust to being paralyzed," I told him. "Just when I think I've got things under control, I go into a tailspin."

"Well, you just take your time, Joni. We'll do anything — anything at all to help, you know that." His sparkling blue eyes and smiling face radiated love and encouragement.

I sighed deeply, then said, "I guess the thing that affects me most is that I'm so helpless. I look around the house here, and everywhere I look I see the things you've built and created. It's really sad to think that I can't leave a legacy like you. When you're gone, you will have left us with beautiful buildings, paintings, sculpture, art. Even the furniture you've made. I can never do any of that. I can never leave a legacy ."

Dad wrinkled his forehead for a moment, then grinned again. "You've got it all wrong. These things I've done with my hands don't mean anything. It's more important that you build character. Leave something of yourself behind. Y'see? You don't build character with your hands."

"Maybe you're right, daddy."

"Of course I am."

"But why does God allow all this? Look at our family. We've had more than our share of heartbreak — first my accident, then Jay's divorce, now — now little Kelly (my niece dying of brain cancer). It's so unfair," I cried.

Daddy put his hands on my shoulders and looked straight into my eyes. "Maybe we'll never know the 'why' of our troubles, Joni. Look — I'm not a minister or a writer — I don't know exactly how to describe what's happening to us. But, Joni, I have to believe God knows what He's doing."

"I don't know," I offered.

"Look, how many times have you heard somebody — we've done it ourselves many times — pray piously: 'Lord, I'm such a sinner. I deserve hell and Your worst condemnation. Thank You for saving me.' We tell God in one breath that we aren't worthy of His goodness. Then, if we happen to run into some trouble or suffering, we get bitter and cry out against God: 'Lord, what are You doing to me?!' Y'see? I think that if we admit we deserve the worst — hell — and then only get a taste of it by having to suffer, we ought to try somehow and live with it, don't you?"

"Do you think I deserved to be paralyzed — that God is punishing me?"

"Of course not, honey. That was taken care of on the cross. I can't say why He allowed this to happen. But I have to believe He knows what He's doing. Trust Him, Joni. Trust Him."

"I'll try," I said half-heartedly.

As spring turned into summer, my emotions got no better. I'd expected a miracle from God at Rancho Los Amigos. I was convinced He'd give me back the use of my hands. When I didn't regain my hands, I felt betrayed. God had let me down.

So I was angry at God. In order to get back at Him, I discovered a way to shut Him out along with the rest of the world. I went into moody, depressive, fantasy "trips." I'd sleep late in order to dream, or I'd take naps most of the day to daydream and fantasize. By concentrating hard, I was able to completely shut out the present and reality.

I tried to recall each vivid detail of every pleasant experience stored in my memory. I focused all my mental energy on living these experiences again and again.

In these fantasies, I recalled every physical pleasure I had had — what it felt like to wear a soft pair of worn Levis, the warm splash of a shower, the caress of wind on my face, the feel of summer sun on skin. Swimming. Riding. The squeaky feel of saddle leather between my thighs. None of these simple pleasures was wrong in itself. But I used them to shut God from my mind.

One day, I was sitting in my wheelchair outside at the ranch, our family's farm, in Sykesville. The friends who had come to visit me had saddled horses and gone on a trail ride. I was feeling sorry for myself, comparing my lot to theirs. Warm summer sunlight glimmered through the branches of big oak trees and danced in bright patterns on the lush grass underneath. I closed my eyes and visualized a similar day a couple years earlier. In my daydream, I was again with Jason, riding horseback together toward the forest, across the fragrant meadows, stopping in a deserted place. I relished memories of unrestrained pleasure, excitement and sensual satisfaction — feelings I knew I had no right to enjoy then or relive now.

When the Holy Spirit convicted me, I rebelled even more. "What right have You to tell me I can't think of these things? You're the One who put me here! I have a right to think about them. I'll never enjoy sensual feelings and pleasure again. You can't take away my memories!"

But the more I thought of these and other experiences, the more withdrawn I became. I was frustrated and bitter and blamed God that these feelings meant so much to me.

I tried to savor and experience other pleasures and memories. When at a friend's house beside their swimming pool, I treasured the experiences I used to have in the water. The liquid pleasure of wetness all around me, of slicing through the clear waters. Of bobbing up from the bottom and feeling the rush of fresh air pouring into my lungs and on my face. Of wet, stringy hair under my head as I lay sunbathing on the warm concrete apron. Of the warm tiny beads of water making small tickly lines while dripping down my drying arms and legs.

I was angry at God. I'd retrieve every tiny physical pleasure from my mind and throw it up to Him in bitterness. I couldn't accept the fact — God's will, they said — that I'd never do or feel these things again. Outwardly, I maintained a facade of cheerfulness. Inwardly, I rebelled.

My fantasy trips became longer and more frequent. And when I ran out of memories which I felt would anger God, I created new ones. I developed wild, lustful, sexual fantasies which I believed would displease Him.

*   *   *   *

Diana came to live with us that summer. At first, she wasn't aware of my "trips." Then she sensed that my fits of depression were getting out of control, as if I were in a trance.

"Joni! Stop it! Wake up!" Diana screamed one day. She shook my shoulders violently. Slowly, I regained my sense of reality.

"W-what?"

"Joni! What's wrong? I was talking to you, and you were just staring past me into space! Are you sick?"

"No. Leave me alone. Just leave me alone!"

"It's not going to help you to avoid reality," Diana said. "You've got to face up to the truth. Don't shut it out. The past is dead, Joni. You're alive."

"Am I?" I replied cynically. "This isn't living."

Periodically she scolded me back from my fantasy trips, but, just as often, I'd leave again. I learned that taking a nap in a darkened room with a window air conditioner was my best "transportation." The hum of the air conditioner was a hypnotic sound which shut out the world; soon I'd be in my trance, capturing past feelings and pleasures.

Finally, I realized I wasn't getting anywhere with my rebellious temper tantrums against God. I began to see it was my way of sinning. Before my accident, sin consisted of the things one did. But now, there was no opportunity for me to give action to sinful thoughts. I began to see that sin was an attitude as much as an act. Before the action, the mind frames the thoughts and attitudes which become the basis for our rebellion against God. I saw that anger, lust, and rebellion, although "merely" attitudes, were sinful. Sin wasn't just all the bad things I did, but was an integral part of my makeup. Although there was no opportunity for me to physically rebel against God, I sinned nonetheless. It was a part of my nature.

I knew that I was being what Paul the apostle described as carnal as opposed to spiritual. I was in an impossible condition — unhappy and unable to please myself or God. "For the carnal attitude is inevitably opposed to the purpose of God, and neither can nor will follow his laws for living. Men who hold this attitude cannot possibly please God" (Rom. 8:7,8).

Or themselves, I reminded myself. I saw that my fits of depression and flights into fantasy were doing nothing except confusing and frustrating me.

I did not understand what God was trying to show me, so I prayed: "Lord, I know now that You have something planned for my life. But I need help understanding Your will. I need help in knowing Your Word. Please, God, do something in my life to help me serve You and know Your Word."

Nine

It was summer, 1969, two years after my diving accident. I thought of the many things which had happened to me during those two incredible years. In taking inventory of my spiritual life, I found it consisted mainly of fantastic highs and lows — but mostly lows. In fact, I'd recently climbed out of the worst depression I'd experienced since the accident. If I didn't receive some help, some mature guidance, I knew I'd sink again. It was only a matter of time.

I made as much progress in rehabilitation as was physically possible. It was evident now I'd never walk again; I'd never get the use of my hands again; I'd forever be paralyzed from the neck down, unable to even care for my own personal needs. It was certain now that I'd be forever dependent on others for every physical comfort or function.

This dependency was enough, in itself, to trigger another bout with depression and self-pity, and I talked about my concerns with Diana.

"I have this tremendous feeling of hopelessness and

worthlessness, Di," I told her. "I'm praying that the Lord
will do something in my life to show me that it has
meaning."

"I've been praying, too, Joni," she replied, adding,
"you know, I'm going to bring a friend over to meet you."

"Who? Why?"

"Steve Estes. You don't know him, but he's at just
the opposite side of things spiritually. He has a love for
the Lord and knowledge of the Scriptures that really
ought to help."

"Sure," I volunteered without much enthusiasm.

"He's a young guy. In fact, he's still in high school."

"High school?! Diana! He's a kid?"

"No — don't judge. Wait 'til you meet him."

Steve Estes came over to the house that evening,
and the minute he walked through the door, he shattered
all my preconceived notions about him.

Steve loomed tall above my wheelchair, and his
piercing green eyes immediately communicated an attitude of warmth and openness. In the introductory conversation which followed, he made me completely at
ease. He evidenced maturity and comfortable self-
assurance, and one of the first things I noticed was his
attitude toward me.

Many people who meet me for the first time seem
awkward and uncomfortable with the chair. It intimi-
dates them or causes them to pity me. It usually takes
several visits and conversations for us to move past the
chair and deal on an ordinary level. Unfortunately, some
people never get to that point, and consequently, I
usually feel self-conscious.

Yet Steve was completely at ease, making me comfortable, too. He talked fast, expressing himself with
animated gestures, and seemed enthusiastic about everything. As we conversed, he began to share biblical concepts — ideas that were exciting to him and stimulating
to me.

"Joni," he said earnestly, "isn't it great what God is
doing in different people's lives today?"

What? Who? Where? I was too embarrassed to ask

the questions as they popped in my mind. It didn't matter. Steve answered them for me.

"Kids are experiencing fantastic things in *Young Life* at Woodlawn. And in our church, we've seen God's Spirit make a lot of people really come alive. One couple was on the verge of divorce — God brought 'em back together. One guy was heavy into dope, and Christ saved him. A girl I know was really messed up inside, and the Lord straightened her out. Man, you should see her today!" The stories came rapid-fire, and I began to see a new reality to God's power. The Lord had worked in people's lives, and the truth and meaning of it spilled over into Steve's experience and then into mine through Steve's recounting.

Steve himself had seen God demonstrate His love and power. Steve's faith, energy, and spiritual maturity were evidently the qualities that made him so different from me. He radiated trust, a love for Christ, and self-assured success. It was amazing to me that a sixteen-year-old could offer so much spiritual insight and wisdom. As a young adult of twenty, I had not come as far. There was something about him, a quality in his life, that I wanted. He radiated confidence, poise, and authority. He spoke convincingly of the Lord and the simple, quiet strength that faith in Christ brings to a life.

"Steve, what you say is like fresh new truth," I said to him excitedly. "Please come back and tell me more."

"Sure, I'd like that."

"Can you help me get what you have? I'm a Christian. But there's so much I don't know about the Lord. You have so much more spiritual knowledge than I do."

"Joni, what would you say if I came over every Wednesday and had a Bible study with you?" he suggested.

"Great," I answered.

Diana was smiling and nodding. "I'm going to be there, too, and maybe Jay and others would like to come. Is that all right?"

"Sure," Steve smiled. It was strange. Here was a boy, just sixteen, planning to teach a group of young adults about the Christian faith. Yet no one questioned his authority or ability to do so. Even then, he had the eloquence and charisma of a spiritual teacher, a minister. Everyone respected him and responded to his qualities of leadership.

Steve enjoyed the challenge. He said, "Joni, your house really makes me feel comfortable. It's like a retreat — the atmosphere makes me feel like we're at L'Abri with Francis Schaeffer."

He sensed that I — and some of the others — had not really mastered some of the basic Christian doctrines — the character of God, deity of Christ, sin, repentance and salvation — and these became the focus of our weekly Bible studies.

"In Ephesians," he explained, "Paul tells us that we have a fantastic heritage: Christ *chose us* even before He made the world. He created us, in His image, for a particular purpose. God wants us to grow and excel, to be successful. A lot of people are confused about what true spirituality is. If a guy knows a lot of Bible verses, he's often thought of as spiritual. But having head knowledge of Bible truth isn't spirituality. True spirituality is putting God's Word into practice — making His truth valid by actually doing what He says and not just pointing to it as a nice standard."

As Steve shared basic Bible doctrine with us, I began to see the shallowness of my own faith and spirituality. My spiritual ups and downs could be charted as easily and accurately as my physical progress. This became something I wanted to overcome, something I wanted to deal with in a positive way. I began to look to the spiritual principles and revolve my life around them for a change.

Alone with God, I recalled how I'd withdrawn from reality and turned my back on Him so often. I confessed, "Lord, I've been wrong — wrong to try and shut You out. Forgive me, God. Thank You for this new understanding of Your Word which Steve has shared. Please forgive me and bring me back to You — back into fellowship with You once more." The Holy Spirit began to convict, then teach me. With each succeeding week, spiritual truth became more real, and I began to see life from God's perspective.

I learned that God's Word is a handbook for sensible living; He doesn't give us instructions without reason.

I saw, in fact, that God tries to warn us in Scripture; for example, sex before marriage is wrong.

There seem to be so many more warnings in the Bible about illicit sex as compared to warnings about other sinful conduct or behavior, such as gossip, envy, lying, and anger. The Bible says of these, "Resist the devil" (James 4:7) — stand and fight and overcome these faults. But as for sexual sin and sensuality, the Bible says, "flee" (1 Cor. 6:18). If I had been obedient and not given in to temptations, I would not have been tormented by longings and desires which now could never be satisfied. They were like an unquenched thirst. No matter how much I shut out reality and lived the experiences in fantasy, it could never be the same. The feelings were shadow substance and unsatisfying.

I had learned some painful lessons from my relationship with Jason. Now I reaped the consequences. I was tortured, but not because I had done something ugly and repulsive. On the contrary, physical love is beautiful and exciting. Yet God knows how it frustrates and torments without the context of marriage. I was lusting after memories. I know other girls who have cried bitter tears over the same thing. They have found that guilt and remorse over sex outside of marriage can cloud and ruin otherwise happy lives and handicap otherwise successful marriages.

But now, with God's help and forgiveness, I repented and put all that behind me. I prayed for His direction and the mental will power to think His thoughts and not wallow in self-pity and lustful memories and fantasies.

I concentrated on the fact that, once and for all, I had to forget the past and concentrate on the present, trusting God, claiming the promise of Scripture that God separates our sins from us forever (Psalm 103:12).

I decided to rid myself of as many reminders of the past as I could. I gave away my cherished hockey and lacrosse sticks, sold my horse, Tumbleweed, and got rid of all the other *things* that tied me to the old memories.

Now I was forced to trust God. I had no alternative but to thank Him for what He was going to do with my future.

As I began to pray and depend on Him, He did not disappoint me. Before, I'd say, "Lord, I want to do Your will — and Your will is for me to get back on my feet or, at least, get my hands back." I was deciding His will for me and rebelling when things didn't turn out as I planned.

Now I wept for all those lost months filled with bitterness and sinful attitudes. I prayed for an understanding of His will for my life. What was God's will for my life? To find out, I had to believe that all that had happened to me was an important part of that plan. I read, "In everything, give thanks, for this is the will of God concerning you." God's will was for me to be thankful in everything? Okay. I blindly trusted that this was truth. I thanked God for what He did and what He was going to do.

As I concentrated on His positive instruction from the Bible, it was no longer necessary to retreat from reality. Feelings no longer seemed important. Fantasies of having physical feeling and touch were no longer necessary because I learned that I was only temporarily deprived of these sensations. The Bible indicates that our bodies are temporal. Therefore, my paralysis was temporal. When my focus shifted to this eternal perspective, all my concerns about being in a wheelchair became trivial.

Steve showed me other evidence in the Bible that God's perspective is different than ours. In Hebrews 12:1, we are encouraged to endure life with patience. Second Corinthians 5:1-5 reminds us that our bodies are the temporary dwellings of our spirits and personalities. Philippians 1:29 says some are called to suffer for Him — maybe even suffer "fiery ordeals," as the author of 1

Peter expressed it: "And now, dear friends of mine, I beg
you not to be unduly alarmed at the fiery ordeals which
come to test your faith, as though this were some abnor-
mal experience. You should be glad, because it means
that you are called to share Christ's sufferings. One day,
when he shows himself in full splendour to men, you will
be filled with the most tremendous joy" (1 Peter 4:12, 13,
PHILLIPS.) Steve took me through the Scriptures and
helped me fit my pain and suffering into this perspective.

"Those who suffer," explained Steve, "should concentrate on doing right and commit their lives and souls
to His care. We should all do that, but the Bible makes a
point of telling those who suffer fiery trials to especially
live for Christ."

In my fantasies and daydreams, I had sought the
reality of past experiences because I wanted to avoid the
truth of the present. Yet, even the present isn't true
reality. There will, one day, be an existence for us that
will be the ultimate in reality and experience, and we can
understand this truth only by faith. What we see by faith
is true reality.

We were all learning and growing through Steve's
late-night sessions at our home. Diana continued to live
with us and went back to college in the fall to study
psychology. One of the "games" she learned in this
course was role-playing to achieve better understanding
of people and various situations.

One night after our study time, we all switched roles
and "walked in each other's shoes" for awhile. Diana and
I changed places. Someone carried me to the sofa while
Diana sat in the wheelchair.

"You know, this is strange," remarked Diana, as
she played me. "You people seem afraid of the wheelchair. Everyone seems to keep his distance. There seems
to be a space around the chair that no one is willing to
intrude on."

"That's interesting," I added. "I was just thinking
how people seem less awkward to me when I'm sitting on
the couch."

We discussed the chair and what it meant to different people. The typical reaction from strangers was condescension toward one who, to them, was somehow inferior. I suppose, as I've said before, some people think that if you are physically handicapped, you are mentally deficient, too.

Diana, Jay, and Dick were so used to the chair that they took a casual attitude toward it. So casual, in fact, that walking with me was often a game. They'd push me one-handed or give me a shove and walk beside the chair. They often did this to puncture the stuffy, provincial attitudes some people have about wheelchairs. For example, the chair is only about two feet wide, but on sidewalks people clear a path wide enough for a car to drive through. Their subtle awkwardness only adds to the confusion and frustration of the person in the chair. It makes them feel clumsy and fat.

People often stare without meaning to, especially when the chair is being wheeled too fast (at least in their opinion). Apparently, popular opinion dictates that a person in a wheelchair should be treated like a load of priceless antiques.

Older women often came up to me in a department store or on the street, clucked their tongues, and said something like, "Oh, you poor, dear, brave, brave girl." I'd smile politely but often felt like telling them my real feelings — which weren't always charming!

However, I came to terms with myself. If others had a problem with the chair, I tried to do everything I could to make them feel at ease. At the Bible studies, I had Dick carry me to the sofa. Out of sight, the chair no longer intimidated people. Sitting, with my legs propped up on an ottoman, I looked like a "normal" person.

What began as a simple experiment in practical psychology became a regular habit for me. I enjoyed being one of the crowd in this way and was glad it made all more comfortable.

Diana tried another experiment in role-playing. This time, I saw my situation as others do. She sat in the chair, and I was on the sofa. "Joni, I'd like a glass of water," Diana said, pretending to be helpless.

Taking her role, I saw something I'd never noticed from my chair. I was annoyed.

"Gee — I'm really engrossed in this TV program. Can you wait until the commercial?" I asked.

"Well — I guess so," sighed Diana.

Everyone smiled knowingly. I said, "Is that the way I really am? Oh, good grief — I'm sorry. I see how selfish I can be without even knowing. I'll try to be more considerate of you guys from now on."

Being out of the wheelchair was also good for my self-confidence as a woman. In the chair, sometimes I felt stiff and awkward, but sitting here on the couch, I felt relaxed and at ease. One evening when we were watching TV, Dick stretched out and put his head in my lap. I managed to take off my arm brace and began to stroke his hair with my hand. Of course, I couldn't feel anything, but Dick could. He relaxed and enjoyed the normal attention of a girl running her fingers through his hair.

These were pleasant moments of growing and learning, offset only by the fact of Kelly's sickness. She was growing weaker almost daily. But her situation, as well as my own, were made easier as I began to grow in faith and understanding.

Steve continued to come, sometimes several times a week. His Bible-based teaching of simple doctrinal truth was becoming a part of my life. Before, I had accepted doctrine pretty much without question. But it was not real in my experience. Its truth had not been tested. In my earlier depression at Greenoaks, I had examined other philosophical and theological points of view. It was no longer possible for me to accept doctrine without question, but even as I questioned, answers were provided. Steve explained Bible truth in such a way that it was as if the Lord spoke directly to me.

I saw Steve's coming into my life as a specific answer to the desperate prayer I had prayed just before I met him.

We discussed the second coming of Jesus Christ. I learned that one day Jesus would return to earth and I'd get a brand-new body. Christ would give me a glorified

body that could do everything I could do before —
probably even more. Some day I would have feelings
again! *I won't be paralyzed forever*.

This new perspective made it unnecessary for me to
retreat into fantasy trips or daydreams any more.

Steve helped me end my cycle of peaks and valleys
of spiritual progress. "Set your heart on things above," he
read from Colossians 3, "and not the passing things of
earth." Since I could see that one day I'd have a renewed
body, it became easy for me to focus my desires on
heavenly, eternal things. I had already lost temporal
things, the use of my earthly body, so it was easy to
accept this truth. Although "condemned" to a wheelchair, I knew one day I'd be free of it.

"Steve," I said to him, "I'm beginning to see the
chair more as a tool than a tragedy. I believe God is going
to teach me something more about this!"

Steve introduced me to the process of putting God's
Word into practice, of acting on His promises and com-
mands. I would read something in the Bible and consciously say, "This is God's will." Intellectually, I understood the meaning of it. Emotionally, I had to put this
new truth to the test, to prove it by my own will. "Yes,
this is God's will," adding, "for me."

"Lord, I'm trusting You to bring me through all this
victoriously," I reminded Him. Scripture took on personal meaning. Job had suffered, so he could speak
convincingly to my needs. Jeremiah had suffered, and I
learned from him, too. Since Paul had endured beatings,
shipwrecks, imprisonment, and ill health, I related to his
sufferings as well. I began to see what the Bible called a
"fellowship of suffering."

I memorized Scripture portions that had great meaning to me. Understanding these passages that spoke to
my needs enabled me to better trust God with my will as
well as my life. Even when distressing or despondent
times came along, I could depend on the fact that "He
knows what He is doing," as daddy frequently said.

Through memorizing God's promises, I learned that
the Lord would take me out of training in this school of

suffering — but in His own good time. The apostle Paul wrote that the key was to keep forever striving. Even he, at the peak of his life and commitment to Christ, admitted that he had not arrived spiritually.

Probably, I thought, *my suffering and training is a life-long process. It will end only when I go to be with Christ.*

There was a lot of catching up for me to do. If life was going to mean anything, I'd have to learn everything I could — not just spiritual truth, but academic understanding as well. I'd have to find a way to make some kind of contribution to society.

Diana and Jay were eager to help me get back into circulation, up-to-date with the outside world. Seeing people and going places was refreshing and stimulating. By now, I was even comfortable in my chair, used to the stares and awkwardness of others. Being outside that summer was a pleasant experience to my senses. Shut in various hospitals for two years, I'd almost forgotten all there was to see, hear, and smell in the outdoors. These experiences saturated my starved senses. But as a result of such sensory shock, I tired easily and was forced to rest after these outdoor trips.

Steve tried to encourage me to verbalize my new understanding — to put this new truth into practice. He asked me to share my faith, the testimony of my Christian experience, with the youth group at his church. The thought of speaking to fifteen teen-agers terrified me. My natural tendency then was to be shy, so when the time came, I was really nervous. I looked out at those polished, self-assured faces and was almost too petrified to speak.

"I . . . uh . . . I'm Joni Eareckson . . . and . . . uh . . . uh . . . ." My mind went blank. *What was I supposed to say?* The teens were polite and didn't break into snickers or mocking. "I . . . I . . . uh . . . I want to tell you . . . uh . . . what Christ means to me. Uh . . . you see . . . He is very . . . uh . . . real to me. I've . . . uh . . . had . . . uh . . . lots of troubles . . . uh . . . but I . . . I mean *He* . . . He's been faithful. And uh . . . I hope you know Him as I do."

My throat was dry, my face was flushed, and I couldn't think of any way to continue, so I merely dropped my gaze and said nothing.

After an awkward, terrifying pause, Steve picked up on what I said. Somehow, he put the pieces together and made sense of it. I was both relieved and impressed that he could salvage the situation.

Later I said firmly, "I never want to do that again as long as I live!"

"Nonsense," Steve countered. "You just need experience. I was the same way the first time a friend asked me to give my testimony at one of his street-corner evangelism meetings."

"Really?"

"I stammered all over the place. I thought my tongue was swollen."

"But I don't have your gift for speaking — your presence of mind. I just can't."

"You should go to college," he said, slapping my knee good-naturedly. "You could attend classes in your wheelchair at the University of Maryland. They have quite a few handicapped people there. You shouldn't have any trouble," Steve suggested.

"Hm-m. Maybe you're right."

He grinned and nodded.

"All right," I conceded, "if Jay and Diana will help, I'll go to college this fall."

In September, I began attending a few classes at the university. Jay or Diana went with me and took notes for me. I signed up for *Oral Interpretation, Voice Diction* and *Public Speaking*. My speeches were related to things I knew about and could discuss easily: relating to people with handicaps, accepting the wheelchair, and my Christian experience.

Slowly, I developed confidence, especially as I saw that people were interested in what I was saying. Deep inside, I sensed that God was preparing me; that somehow, someday, I'd be able to use what I was learning.

At the same time, I began to understand spiritual

truth in meaningful ways. This new understanding gave me victory over past sin, temptation, and depression. God had given me the means to control my sinful nature when I realized the importance of His reality and the present.

The fantasies ended. Forever. With God's complete fulfillment, I didn't need to relive memories from the past. I had come to the place where my body no longer needed the sensations I once thought so terribly important. God had taken me beyond the need for feeling and touching. Yet, He saw to it that, whenever possible, I could enjoy such things as the feel of a cashmere sweater on my cheek, a hug from someone I care about, the reassuring movement of a rocking chair, and the sensations He brought everytime I went outside — wind, sun, even rain on my face. And I was grateful for all He gave.

Ten

In February, 1970, my niece Kelly died of the brain tumor that had kept her in constant pain for a year. Her death underscored to me the importance of each individual soul.

I was just beginning to get a handle on a positive spiritual frame of reference myself, so Kelly's progress in faith, though she was only five, was encouraging and helpful to me as I saw the reality of God's love and power at work in her tiny life. Her tragedy brought us closer as a family and closer to the Lord.

We had all accepted the inevitability of Kelly's death, and we had peace about it; yet, this did not mean that the agony of losing her did not take its toll on us or that we did not ever ask "Why, God?"

Kelly's mother, my sister Linda, suffered the most. Soon after Kelly became ill, Linda's husband left and divorced her. This left her with two sons and Kelly to support, along with facing Kelly's death. Her world seemed to be collapsing around her, and for a long time she didn't want to face it.

Through Kelly's death and my own paralysis, I was learning that there was nothing but unhappy frustration in trying to second-guess God's purposes. *Why God? Why did Kelly die? Why was I paralyzed? Why was someone else alive and healthy?* There was no reason apart from the overall purposes of God.

We aren't always responsible for the circumstances in which we find ourselves. However, we *are* responsible for the way we respond to them. We can give up in depression and suicidal despair. Or, we can look to a sovereign God who has everything under control, who can use the experiences for our ultimate good by transforming us to the image of Christ (2 Cor. 3:18).

God engineered circumstances. He used them to prove Himself as well as my loyalty. Not everyone had this privilege. I felt there were only a few people God cared for in such a special way that He would trust them with this kind of experience. This understanding left me relaxed and comfortable as I relied on His love, exercising newly learned trust. I saw that my injury was not a tragedy but a gift God was using to help me conform to the image of Christ, something that would mean my ultimate satisfaction, happiness — even joy.

Steve, in one of our fellowship study sessions, compared my life to the experience of the apostle Paul: "I want you to know, my brothers, that what has happened to me has, in effect, turned out to the advantage of the gospel" (Phil. 1:12).

I reflected over this concept one evening as Steve crossed the room to stir the fire in the fireplace. He reminded me, "Joni, what is happening to you will advance God's cause! Paul had his prison chains; you have your chair. You can rejoice in suffering because He is allowing you to suffer on His behalf." Steve then sat down and stretched his frame into the overstuffed chair, thumbing through his Bible. " 'You are given, in this battle,' " he read, " 'the privilege not merely of believing in Christ but also suffering for his sake' (Phil. 1:29)."

It was exciting to think that what had happened to me could indeed "turn out to the advantage of the gos-

Joni • 155

pel." I began to share my faith with more people in a positive context, and I saw that the Word of God could not be bound and chained, even if I was (2 Tim. 2:10).

Now, as each successive problem arose, it came in a context I understood. I merely trusted God. I reminded myself that all things came into my life according to Andrew Murray's formula: by God's appointment, in His keeping, under His training, for His time. And I had His promise that He would not heap upon me more than I could bear.

As I began to see that circumstances are ordained of God, I discovered that truth could be learned only through application.

In 2 Thessalonians, I read, "In everything give thanks." But sometimes I didn't want to give thanks. Emotionally, it was something I just didn't feel like doing. Yet, I could give thanks with my will, if not my feelings.

"After all," I reasoned one day to Steve, "for two years, I woke up every morning in a hospital. If for no other reason than that, I can give thanks that I'm no longer there."

So I began a habit of giving thanks, even when I didn't feel thankful. After awhile, a curious thing happened. I began to feel thankful!

"Your paralysis could even be a blessing," observed Steve during one of our times together.

"A blessing?"

"Sure."

"I don't know about that," I admitted. "I've come a long way just to accept my accident as something God has allowed for my ultimate good. But I don't really feel it's a blessing yet."

During the weeks ahead, I read more and more on the subject of God's sovereignty. It truly was a reassuring doctrine. As its light flooded my intellect and mind, it brightened my spirit and self-image. I felt secure, safe. God had control of everything in my life.

That spring, Steve and his parents went to a seminar where the value of "self" was explained in biblical terms.

Steve shared these concepts with me one afternoon when he stopped by with some books he wanted me to read.

"Joni, you must know by now the value God places on you," he said as he plopped them on the table.

"Yes, I suppose so. Why?"

"Well, I think you're still hung up on your self-image."

"Hung up on my self-image? What do you mean?"

"You're always putting yourself down — always on the defensive," he replied.

Steve was right, of course. I'd still look at healthy, active people — attractive people — enjoying themselves around me. Everyone I compared myself to came out best. I'd even lose out when I compared myself to a mannequin!

"But that's the same for everyone if we let society determine our value," Steve explained as he sat down on the piano bench. "We always lose when we evaluate ourselves according to someone else's ideas or standards. And there are as many standards as there are people. A jock measures you by your athletic ability; a student by your brains; a steady by your looks. It's a losing battle," he said, striking a sour piano chord for added emphasis. "We have to forget about what people say or think and recognize that God's values are the only important ones."

It was true. God knew that I had hands and feet and arms and legs that did not work. He knew what I looked like. And none of these things really mattered. What counted was that I was His workmanship created in His image. And He wasn't finished with me (Eph. 2:10).

In the days that followed, I thanked Him for "me" — whatever I was in terms of mind, spirit, personality — and even body. I thanked Him for the way I looked and for what I could and could not do. As I did, the doctrine of His sovereignty helped everything fall into place, like a jigsaw puzzle.

Not only was there purpose to my life at this point, but there was an iceberg of potential as well — 10 percent above the surface, 90 percent below. It was an exciting thought — an entire new area of my life and personality not even developed yet!

"Joni, I learned this concept from an illustration Bill Gothard (*Institute in Basic Youth Conflicts*) uses. He says our lives are like paintings which God is making. Often we jump off the easel, grab a brush, and want to do things ourselves. But when we do this, we only get a bad copy of the masterpiece He intended for our lives."

Steve added to this thought. "Joni, your body — in the chair — is only the frame for God's portrait of you. Y'know, people don't go to an art gallery to admire frames. Their focus is on the quality and character of the painting."

This made sense. I could relax and not worry so much about my appearance. God was "painting" me in just the perfect way so I could enhance the character of Christ within. This gave a whole new perspective to the chair. Once it had been a terrible burden, a trial for me. Then, as I saw God working in my life, it became only a tool. Now, I could see it as a blessing. *For the first time in my paralyzed life, it was indeed possible for the wheelchair to be an instrument of joy in my life.*

Eleven

With new understanding and a more positive self-image came a concern for my appearance. Jay and Diana helped me fix my hair and make-up, and we learned how to buy clothes that fit me better. For example, Jay discovered that by buying my slacks three inches too long, they hung properly and didn't hitch up above my ankles when I sat in the chair.

I was at the point in my life where I was actually satisfied with my situation. I had begun by thanking God with my will. Now I could do it with my emotions. My wheelchair was now a comfortable part of my life.

In the summer of 1970, Diana, Jay, Sheri Pendergrass (a thirteen-year-old neighbor), and I drove to Philadelphia to attend the Gothard seminar which Steve recommended highly. The sessions further helped to crystallize my thinking on all that had been happening to me. One seminar section dealt with "Sources of Irritation," and I learned that God allows certain circumstances to come into our lives almost as a rasp to file down the rough edges, to smooth us into gems.

"Irritations come through circumstances and people," Diana reminded us after one of the sessions.
"That's why it's important not only to endure, but to
respond with a godly attitude."

"Yeah," I said quietly. "I guess I've really been
slow to see this truth. It's not enough for me to put up with
all that God permits by way of suffering. I need to use my
situation for His glory — to let these situations make me
more Christlike."

"That's not easy," Jay observed.

"Boy, that's for sure," Sheri added. " 'Respond with
a godly attitude.' That's what it says. But it sure isn't all
that easy!"

"Well, let's put it to the test," Diana suggested.
"When sources of irritation come along, let's not give in
to them and let Satan get a victory over our emotions and
feelings."

During the next intermission, it seemed God gave
me an excellent opportunity to test this principle concerning sources of irritation. Since I'm confined to a
wheelchair, I have to drink a lot of liquids to force my
kidneys to function properly in removing body wastes.
Consequently, I have a catheter attached to a leg bag
which collects urine and has to be emptied periodically.
Sheri was taking care of me that day, and she emptied the
bag but forgot to clamp it again. Soon after that a man
seated in front of us looked down, then turned around.

"Miss, I think something is wrong — " he said.

"Oh, no!" I looked down and saw a puddle running
down the aisle. I flushed with embarrassment and a sick,
sinking feeling. I began to feel irritation developing —
irritation at Sheri, at the whole routine of my chair, at
many things. Then I remembered the lesson just learned.
It seemed we all saw in this humiliating incident an
object lesson which proved we really did learn the truth
of that point.

Other seminar truths also made a significant impact
on my life. I saw anew the importance of my family in my
life.

The fact that I am single and handicapped makes

me especially aware of my dependence upon my folks and my sisters. Yet the principles are the same for everyone. It is no mistake that our lives and experiences are what they are — even the number of brothers and sisters we have and who our parents are. They are all part of God's purposes and plans.

That is certainly true in my life. Each of my sisters is special to me, but each is different, with varied skills, abilities, and personalities.

"If I can't learn to love each one of my sisters for themselves alone, how can I ever hope to love someone else with their traits?" I wondered with my friends.

"That sure makes sense," said Diana.

"Yeah," added Jay.

"Jay — " I said slowly, "I'm just beginning now to see how little I've loved and appreciated you, Kathy, and Linda. I've really taken your love for granted. You pick up after my friends, cook, clean, and never complain. I'm sorry I've been so thick. Maybe I can have my friends clean up after themselves when they visit — I mean like put the dirty dishes and glasses in the dishwasher after we have snacks."

Jay smiled and hugged me. I had touched a sensitive spot, and she seemed appreciative.

"And I've really been kind of insensitive to Kathy and Butch since their recent marriage. I mean, well, she's a schoolteacher, and I guess I don't know enough about her work and problems to really relate to her. I'm going to make an effort to change. Will you guys pray for me?"

"Sure, Joni. We need to pray for each other 'cause we all want to change," said Sheri.

My greatest insight from these seminar sessions was learning that solid relationships have to be worked at. I promised the Lord (and myself) to be generally more considerate of my family and more thoughtful of their needs. It became clear to me that what happened with my family was, in a sense, a proving ground for the consistency of my dealings with others out there in the world. It was harder to be real, to be consistent, at home — but if it worked there, it would work anywhere!

Working things out through love is the standard by which God measures the success of relationships. The principle is the same whether we're talking about a husband-wife relationship, a roommate relationship, a mother-daughter relationship, a father-son relationship, or any relationship in which God has placed us.

Before, because of my injury and unique handicap, my world revolved around me. I enjoyed the attention and things people did for me. But now I could see the selfishness in such a situation, and I consciously tried to change — to make my world revolve around others.

In so doing, I learned not to take my friends and family for granted, not to expect them to always do things for me, but to be genuinely appreciative for all that they did, for all their favors. As a result of this conscious effort to be consistent in all my relationships, especially with my family, my friends who came to visit saw I was the same Joni Eareckson to both.

One friend said once, "Well, I think you can let your hair down with your family and be yourself and not worry about what others think."

I disagreed. "Uh-uh. That's the same as giving us freedom to sin. We both know guys who are pious on Sunday but live like the devil the rest of the week. It's like saying, 'I don't really care enough about my family to show them love and patience. They're not worth it.' I think that if Christ is to be real in my life as I relate to others, He first has to be real in my attitudes with my family."

I saw God continually "working out my salvation." He helped me deal with my past, for which He had forgiven me through Christ's death and resurrection. Then I saw Him effectively at work in the present. Although still apprehensive, I knew God was working in my life to save me not only from the past penalty of sin, but from its present power. Finally, I knew His Spirit was busy within me, trying to create a Christlike character in my life. Therefore, I could trust Him for the future and the full expression of His redemption which I would realize in the life to come.

My art had no special place in my life during this period of growth. Although I often relaxed by drawing or dabbling in creative things, art didn't really fit into the overall scheme of things. It was just a simple pleasure I pursued for fun, as was my interest in music.

During the summer of 1970, I met Dick Rohlfs and brothers Chuck and Craig Garriott. After we got to know one another during Steve's Bible studies, Dickie, Dick, Craig, Diana, and I formed a singing group. Often our house was filled with music and people. Craig's bass guitar resounded off the cathedral ceilings of our living room, and the music got so loud we had to open the windows. Many times, mom and dad sat on the steps at the edge of the room, clapping and singing along with us, often until after midnight when we were all too hoarse to continue. We were pretty good — good enough to sing for *Young Life* and *Youth for Christ* clubs, churches, and other functions.

About this same time, I was asked to work as a counselor with a *Young Life* club in nearby Randalls-town. I agreed and began to share with the high school kids the excitement and enthusiasm of the wonderful things God was now doing in and through my life. The spiritual lessons and values I'd learned were of importance to every Christian, and I was concerned that these eager, bright, young teen-agers might learn the lessons God had taught me without having to go through the same suffering I had.

I understood their lives and experiences. Just a few years earlier, I, too, had been restless, uncertain, searching. I could relate to them on many levels, and I understood them from the perspective of their own "handicaps" — shyness, being overweight, not having a date, braces on their teeth, divorced parents, and many other "handicaps."

"God's Word is true," I told a group of the girls. "I know it's true because I've experienced it. I've found it to be so." They listened attentively as I shared my emotional failures and spiritual successes. Many of them came to the Bible studies we'd hold out at the ranch in Sykesville. To break the ice, we dreamed up all kinds of fun projects for the girls who came, ranging from simple pajama parties to ridiculous games designed to bring the girls together not only for the fun, but for the spiritual lessons which followed.

That summer, Jay and I went to the *Young Life* camp in Colorado as counselors. The camp, named *Frontier Ranch*, was situated in the central Rocky Mountains. It was exciting to be there — the first time back in the crisp mountain air since before my accident. I basked in the sun and Rocky Mountain beauty, with fragrant pine-laden breezes. Of course, I couldn't participate in the hikes, horseback riding, running or mountain climbing, and the kids felt badly about this. But when they saw I wasn't unhappy and was content to watch them, they seemed more relaxed.

"Don't you wish you could do these things with us?" one young girl asked me.

"Well, not really. I'm just happy to be out here — out in God's outdoors where I can meditate on His goodness and greatness and pray. I'm not upset because I can't keep up with you girls. After all, some of the other counselors can't keep up in everything you want to do either!"

Gradually the girls accepted me and my chair and tried to involve me as much as possible in their activities. And although they knew I couldn't check on them after curfew, they never took advantage of my handicap and always treated me as a normal human being.

In the club meetings, outings, and Bible studies, we challenged the kids to live for Christ. We also helped them envision success — to relate their God-given gifts and abilities to service for Christ and His kingdom.

One girl, for example, took an interest in helping me. Debbie (who has since married Chuck Garriott) became a physical therapist. I don't think I necessarily planted that idea in her mind, but I did provide an experience for her in which she felt needed and important by using her talent to help someone.

Towards the end of summer, we had a going-away party for Steve. It was a time of mixed emotions. I was happy for him that he was going off to Bible college, but I was sad to think that our spiritual sharing would end.

"It's not going to end," Steve reassured me. "Look, I read somewhere that 'nothing of God dies when a man of God dies.' You can also interpret that to mean 'no one is indispensable.' God doesn't leave when His children move away. Joni, you just keep your focus on Christ, not me."

"But, Steve, I've learned so much from you this past year. You've introduced me to Paul, to the great Christian writers. I'm excited for you — and I'll pray for you at Columbia Bible College — but I'm going to miss you. God has used you to turn my life completely around. I've grown dependent on you as my spiritual leader this year."

"Listen — that's not true, Joni. God just used me. The Holy Spirit was your real instructor. Keep on with Christ. Keep memorizing the Word. He'll be faithful, Joni."

Steve left for college and, in spite of his reassurances and many letters, I still missed him. Yet, he was right in that I could still grow and learn by looking to the Holy Spirit for direction and understanding.

Twelve

That fall of 1970, my life began to take on interesting dimensions. With Steve away at Bible college and other friends at college or getting married, I became aware once more that there were no prospects for my own marriage. I began to deal realistically with the concept that God's plan for me was singleness. It was a disappointment to read Christian books on the subject, since most of them assume that the single woman must prepare to one day be a married woman. Few, if any, gave realistic, practical advice for a woman confronting singlehood as a life-long reality.

I still had deep-seated and highly emotional reservations about giving up Dick. I felt I was doing the proper thing. I had no right to marry — unless God returned that right as a special grace. That seemed remote and highly unlikely.

So I tried to accept my single role without bitterness or bad attitudes.

I often sang or was a bridesmaid at the weddings of my friends — and even caught the bridal bouquet several times. These occasions brought forth feelings and emotions long forgotten — or so I thought until they surfaced.

I suppose, deep down, I was secretly wishing for the right man to come along — the man who could handle my handicap and the chair. *Lord, You know I'm content in my present state, but I suppose I'll always wonder if You have a man planned for me.*

*   *   *   *

Many of my friends were married now, and I often found it difficult to relate to them. Their interests were different; they were caught up in establishing a home and family — too busy with their own lives taking on new directions to be involved in the interests we once had together. By now I was mature enough to accept this as a natural development in our friendships, so I wasn't resentful or bitter. But I did feel separate, alone.

I wondered whether God would ever bring into my life a man capable of loving me for myself and willing to spend his life with me. Could I ever be happy single? Hadn't I gone through enough? Would God try me further by allowing me to remain single all my life?

These questions fed my emotional insecurity, and loneliness swept over me.

"God," I prayed, "please bring someone into my life to bridge this emptiness."

Why? Isn't My grace sufficient for you?

I knew I was asking for my desires and not God's will. But, after all, didn't Jesus say, "Ask whatever you will in my name and I'll give it to you"?

Shortly after that, at a *Young Life* leadership meeting, I met Donald Bertolli, a friend of Dick's.

"Don's from the tough area of town — Pimlico — and works with kids from the street," the leader said, as he introduced Don. "Our church, Arlington Presbyterian, sponsors this work among the poor minority kids there."

Donald was a handsome, rugged man of Assyrian-Italian descent, with large, dark brown eyes. He seemed wound like a spring — full of energy and strength.

Although he was older than most of us — twenty-seven to my twenty-one, for example — he seemed to enjoy the time together with us.

When he spoke, it was often with a question. His voice had cracks and a roughness that reflected a streetwise background. He distrusted pat answers and persisted to get at the real core of truth. His voice was also hesitant, somewhat shy, almost as if he was afraid to share his inner thoughts aloud.

As he questioned, he'd stop to reflect. He gave intense concentration to what was said, but didn't seem easily swayed or convinced.

When someone acknowledged, "But that's the way it is," Donald interrupted with, "That's a cop-out! Nothing has to be just because that's the way it's always been before."

I was impressed not only with his good looks and intelligence, but with his mature Christian testimony and strong character.

Donald came over to me after the meeting ended and chatted briefly. In those few moments, I learned we had a great deal in common. He talked about his interests — athletics, God, and Christian service.

"Joni, let's talk some more. Can I see you again?"

"Sure — come on over any time."

It was a standard invitation. I'd extended it to many others who asked to talk with me, so I didn't really expect him to be at our door first thing the next morning. But he was.

"Someone's here to see you. I don't know who he is, but he sure is good looking!" said Jay in hushed tones, waking me.

"Who? What time is it?" I yawned.

"Nine o'clock. He says his name is Don."

"Tell him I'll be out in awhile. Just give me a minute to wake up." Being a late riser, this was the time I usually woke in the morning.

Jay went into the other room and chatted pleasantly for a moment or two, then excused herself to come and help me get up, dress, and ready for the new day.

"Good morning!" I said cheerfully a half-hour later when Jay wheeled me into the other room.

"Hi!" Donald said. He bounded out of the chair and came toward me. "Hope I'm not intruding — but you did invite me, didn't you?"

"Of course I invited you. My day usually starts around this time, so you're not intruding."

Donald began to talk. When he stopped for breath, it was noon. I hadn't had breakfast and was hungry, but he showed no signs of ending the visit.

"Donald, would you like to stay for lunch?" I asked.

"Hey, I'd love to — if it's no bother."

Jay prepared a lunch and listened while we talked. Actually, I did most of the listening, too. I learned about Donald, his family, how he met the Lord, all about his work among the young black kids in Pimlico, and his ideas for Christian service.

"Donald, would you like to stay for dinner?" asked Jay later.

"Hey, I'd love to — if it's no bother."

We talked through dinner and finally, after dinner, Donald rose to leave.

"Can I come back to see you?" he asked.

"Uh — well," I hesitated, thinking he might be at the door in the morning again. "Tomorrow I have classes at college."

"Let me take you."

"Uh — that's okay, Donald. Thanks, but Jay usually takes me. She knows my routine and needs."

"Okay. Well, I've really enjoyed this visit. Let's do it again."

"I'd like that."

The next day, he met us outside the school and spent the remainder of the day with us. At first, I was a little put off by what seemed an overbearing approach. But by the third day (when he came to the ranch again), I was beginning to like him.

At the next *Young Life* leadership session, he was there, smiling, handsome, and personable. During the course of the evening, Diana and I got into a friendly but heated discussion over some theological insignificance, and many of the younger people there chose sides and joined in. Yet, Donald seemed to withdraw. That was strange, since there were several new Christians at the study. I was sure he would speak up and end the confusion which Diana and I had raised in our debate.

Finally, the study ended. Donald rose and said to me, "Joni, before you turn in tonight, look up 2 Timothy 2:14 and read it. I think it'll really speak to your heart."

Then he left.

Excitedly, I looked for my Bible. "Hey, great! Why didn't he tell me about this verse before?" I said, thinking it was a verse to help me convince Diana that I was right. Someone found the verse and read it to me: "Remind your people of things like this, and tell them as before God not to fight wordy battles, which help no one and may undermine the faith of some who hear them."

I was stunned by the impact of that truth and convicted that we had argued about such a trifle that evening. Most of all, though, I felt badly about my own immaturity.

However, the other side of the coin immediately became clear to me. I was impressed with Donald's maturity, sensitivity, and wisdom. I saw in him a man of authority, and he became more and more attractive to me. I thought of him often during the next few days.

At our next meeting, we exchanged greetings and immediately shared how much each of us was beginning to mean to the other.

"Joni, before I became a Christian, where I come from it's every man for himself — dog eat dog, y'know? I've been in Christian circles for several years now, though. But, it's funny — I've never experienced people showing love before. I'm really attracted to you."

"I like you, too, Donald. No one's ever come to me before and started a friendship so easily. Usually they're put off by my chair. It takes a while to get past my handicap. When they get to know me, they forget the chair. But with you — well, it's like you never saw the chair in the first place."

"Joni, I don't know — I guess it's my background — but I can't cover my feelings and emotions. I won't try to hide behind some jive talk or hypocrisy. I won't ever con you," he told me.

"I'm glad you don't beat around the bush. I like it when a person isn't afraid to say what's on his mind," I replied.

We saw a great deal of each other in the weeks and months which followed. Before summer ended, Donald took me to Ocean City. He stood beside my wheelchair on the boardwalk as we inhaled the fresh, salty ocean air and soaked in the sounds of gulls and waves crashing.

Old memories returned — the feel of sand between my toes and the exhilarating wetness of the surf splashing over me in the water. I sighed and sat in my chair, prepared to watch Don swim for my vicarious enjoyment.

But suddenly, seeming to sense my mood, he began pushing me off the boardwalk into the sand. The wheels bogged down, but he was strong and virtually plowed furrows toward the wet sand near the water's edge. Here it was packed and traction was easier.

Donald didn't stop! He plunged ahead with a controlled recklessness until I was all the way out in the water — up to my legs.

"Don-ald! What are you doing?" I screamed. The wheelchair was completely into the rolling surf. I was both shocked and thrilled at the impromptu excitement.

People on the beach looked at this ridiculous sight, uncertain as to whether they should intervene and stop this "madman" who was "trying to drown the poor crippled girl." My laughter and obvious enjoyment reassured them, however, and they returned to their own preoccupations.

Donald picked me up and carried me out into the breakers. I couldn't feel it, but I knew my heart was pounding madly.

After this Ocean City experience, I was floating on air. Donald made me feel "normal" for the first time since my accident. The wheelchair was no object to get in his way — there was no pity or uncomfortable, awkward uncertainty. He treated me as he would any woman he liked. He was strong, but always gentle, giving me assurance. I knew he'd never let anything happen to me.

Donald also made me feel attractive, feminine. For the first time since my accident, I felt like a woman — appealing to someone who saw qualities of beauty in me.

As the season changed, Donald took me on picnics and trail hikes. He'd push my wheelchair as far as he could on the trail. When the path narrowed too much, he'd simply fold up the chair, pick me up, and carry me to the top of the hill. There he'd spread out a blanket, and we'd have a picnic lunch and view the scenic beauty.

We'd talk for hours, sharing God's Word and what each of us had learned through our individual Christian experiences. These were romantic, enjoyable, spiritual times. And each one brought us closer together.

I began to worry about my growing deep affection for Donald and where such feelings might lead me. I knew I had to guard against becoming too involved, too close, guard against caring too much for him. Anything more than a "platonic" relationship would be out of the question.

By the spring of 1971, we were spending a great deal of time together. He often took me with him to his work on the street. As I watched him minister to the kids, I was even more impressed with him as a person. His strengths made him a dominant individual in every situation he faced. He was confident without being domineering.

Against my better judgment, I was allowing myself to become even closer to him, allowing strong emotional ties.

One day as I was outside drawing a picture in the warm, spring sunlight, Donald leaned over and said softly, "Joni, I love you."

Caught up in the creative and spiritual expressions of my drawing, I said, "I love you, too, Donald," with the same inflection I'd use in saying, "Yes, you're a good friend, too, Donald."

"Joni, I don't think you understand — " he paused

and looked intently into my eyes. "Joni — I'm falling in love with you!"

He bent down to take my face in his hands and kiss me. I was frightened. I couldn't kiss him without weighing the importance of my actions. A kiss from another woman might be just a casual display of affection. But for me, in a wheelchair, it called for mutual commitment. I didn't want to impose such a commitment on Donald without letting him think through the consequences.

"Look, Donald, this is — "

"But I love you."

"I — I don't know." I was afraid. A relationship based on anything but friendship would be out of the question. "You — uh — we're not able to handle it."

As confident and self-assured as Donald was with me, I felt deep inside that even he could not ultimately deal with the complications my paralysis presented.

Later, I mentioned the episode to Diana and Jay. As I shared my emotional feelings, they both became over-protective and guarded.

"I don't think you should get serious with Donald," urged Jay. "You'll both get hurt."

"Joni," added Diana, "I know he's sincere and doesn't take advantage of you. I know he's good to be with, and I can tell he really likes you. But love? Wow, that's something else altogether. Be careful. Please be careful."

Thirteen

That same summer I had met Don, Diana had met and fallen in love with a young man named Frank Mood. Diana and Frank were married in June, 1971, and moved into a house near our family ranch in Sykesville. About the same time, Jay invited me to come and live with her at the family ranch. Jay lived in a two-hundred-year-old stone and timber building that had once been slaves' quarters well over a century ago and which dad had remodeled. It was a quaint, two-bedroom cottage on a knoll overlooking the picturesque river valley. Living at the ranch would mean that I could spend time with Jay, Diana and Frank, or Kathy and Butch, and they all would share in caring for my needs.

When it was decided I would live with Jay, dad added a wing to her house. It was a big room, planned for the same kind of traffic and entertainment of friends as the house in Woodlawn. In the corner was a beautiful fireplace. The outside walls had picture windows to let in light and scenic beauty. The inner walls were lined with wood paneling he made by hand. The center of the big room was dominated by a huge oak dining-conference table where all our activities seemed to center.

I had loved the ranch as a girl; I loved it even more now. It brought a sense of tranquillity and beauty into my life.

Donald liked the ranch, too, and he spent more and more of his time there with me. Together we took trips to Ocean City, went on picnics, on hiking trips in the hills, and other outings. I never worried about going anywhere with him because I knew he could handle any emergency. He was strong enough to carry me by himself; he helped me eat and drink; he emptied my leg bag, and he could position me in my chair.

I was relaxed and at ease with him. He was never put off by the physical aspects of my handicap and never bothered by the wheelchair itself. He treated me normally; he joked, played, challenged, and provoked me as he would if I were not paralyzed.

If anyone can handle the physical and psychological problems of my handicap, Donald can, I thought. The possibility of a man coming into my life, not as a brother in Christ, but as a romantic interest, both frightened and excited me.

Diana and Jay again warned me not to get romantically involved with Donald. Later, Diana told me of a similar "Dutch uncle" talk she had had with Donald on the same subject.

"Donald, I want you to know that Jay and I are concerned about what's happening with you and Joni," Diana had cautioned.

"Concerned?" he asked.

"Yes. You're getting too serious. Have you thought about what this means to Joni?"

"Yes, I have," Donald replied. "I've thought very seriously about what's happening. I wouldn't lead her on if I weren't serious. Diana, I'm falling in love with Joni."

"But — Donald — uh — usually when two people fall in love, they make plans to marry and spend the rest of their lives together."

"Yes, I know. Diana, I know all the problems. I've

thought and prayed about all the problems of such a relationship. I know the consequences if we'd get married. But I can handle it. I'd marry her now if she'd have me!"

When Diana shared her conversation with me, she still wasn't sure. "Joni, I'm really happy for you — but — "

"I know, Diana," I reassured her. "I'm filled with mixed emotions, too. On one hand, I'm sure I love him, and I believe, really believe, that if anyone can handle such a marriage, Donald can. On the other hand, I think it's probably impossible for anyone to cope with it. I — I guess it's that doubt I want to protect myself from."

"Do you love him?"

"Yes, I guess I do. It's scary. But, y'know, I like it!"

As our love grew, I kept weighing the significance of such a relationship.

"We're talking about a terribly important commitment, Donald," I said one day as we were driving to a softball game.

"I know. But we're able to handle it, Joni. We're both independent and resourceful spirits. We can do it."

"But marriage — "

"Is no more out of the question than anything else. I could take care of you — bathe you, fix meals, clean the house. We could get a mobile home so everything is compact and easy to handle. When we can afford it, we could get something better — maybe even some cleaning and cooking help. Meanwhile, I could do it. I could take care of you."

We pulled into the park and stopped near the ball diamond. "But I could never really be happy not being able to serve you fully as a woman. I want to fix you meals, care for your needs. I want to be able to express my love and tenderness fully as a woman."

"Well, I'm a liberated male, I guess. My cooking and caring for you won't detract from my masculinity. And as for sex, well — I've heard it said that it's overrated," he smiled. "Don't worry, Joni. Sex isn't that important. I can handle it."

I was unsure. I felt that sex was, indeed, an important part of marriage. But as I weighed the problem, I thought, *Perhaps Donald is right. After all, if he says he can cope with the problems, I believe him. I've learned to trust his judgment.* I also recalled the lectures given to paraplegics and quadriplegics at Rancho Los Amigos during my rehabilitation there. Doctors instructed us on the possibility of lovemaking — even the fact of being able to have children. Our bodies being paralyzed only meant we had no physical feelings; function was not impaired.

"But you know — I can't feel anything," I reminded Donald. "I don't think that I could really be free to satisfy you. I'd feel trapped by my body, not able to express love and tenderness in ways that would meet your needs. We'd both be turned off by a lifetime of mutual frustration!"

"I said it's not important." Then he took my chair out and lifted me into it, continuing, "People live with worse problems. Besides, we'll work it out."

"I — I don't know. I suppose. If you tell me that you can handle that kind of a marriage, I guess I believe you. I — I suppose I could commit myself to you."

Donald smiled tenderly and nodded. Oblivious to the players on the ball diamond, he bent his face toward me in a kiss. This time, I felt his gesture was rich with mutual commitment and meaning. And this time, I returned his kiss with the deep feelings of giving and trust. My head swam with emotion and excitement as he wheeled me toward the bleachers.

This is too good to be true! I thought. *Donald came into my life at exactly the time Diana, my best friend, is going out of my life for marriage and a family of her own.*

God had brought me someone who really cared about me; someone who sincerely believed in the idea that we could spend the rest of our lives together.

"This is God's highest plan for me," I reasoned with Jay when I returned home that evening. "It's that 'most excellent thing' He has reserved for my life! After all these years of patience, in accepting my lot as a hand-

icapped person — and especially an unmarried person
— God is now rewarding my patience and trust. Donald
is the answer to my prayers!"

I was deliriously happy. Even when I was on my
feet, I'd never been this happy. We both talked excitedly
about sharing our lives together, about serving Christ
together.

As I thought of this and what God's will on the
matter was, I looked to Scripture. Everywhere I turned,
verses leaped from the pages to confirm my thoughts.

"No good thing will the Lord withhold from those
who walk uprightly.

"Every good gift and every perfect gift is from
above.

"Donald is my 'good thing,' my 'perfect gift' from the
Lord," I told Jay.

She shook her head. "I don't know, Joni. Don't read
in more than is there."

I wrote a song expressing my thoughts and gave the
poem to Donald:

> I woke up this morning to the sight of light —
>   bright, yellow, mellow —
>   and I thought it only right
> To praise my God for morning — and you.
>
> Lying here, teasing my mind with sleep
>   in mist-muted colors —
>   Smiling, I keep on
> Praising my God for the evening — and you.
>
> A trail of thoughts giving way to dreams
>   of past and future —
>   that finally it seems that I
> Praise my God for the present — and you!

I was so happy. I'd never imagined anyone would
love me as a woman while I was in the chair. I suppose
that's why I was so thrilled and excited when it really
happened.

*   *   *   *

Just before Christmas that year, Donald and I had our first argument. We'd been spending a lot of time together, and I began to become possessive. I was even upset when he had to work. I wanted to spend all my time with him; I wanted his life to center around me.

When pretty, young girls from church or youth groups came to visit, I was jealous when he laughed and chatted with them. I became envious that I wasn't on my feet to compete for his attention.

It became more and more difficult for me to concentrate on God's Word and have a devotional or prayer life. It was hard to discuss spiritual things after bickering about "why didn't you come and see me last night?" As a result, my prayer life dwindled to nothing.

My feelings for him became almost all-consuming.

Donald reacted vocally and forcefully. He reminded me that I was acting foolish — like a possessive schoolgirl. I told him I was sorry, that I wouldn't be so demanding of his time and affections; but for some reason, I'd still give in to these unreasonable fears.

Donald decided we both needed a vacation from each other, so he planned to take a trip to Europe in January, 1972. I resisted, taking his plans as a personal rebuke, as if he wanted to get away from me for some reason.

"I just think we need some time to ourselves, Joni," he explained. "Don't read anything else into it at all. Besides," he added, "I've wanted to take this trip for a long time. The guys and I will probably never have an opportunity like this again."

Dickie and Dave Filbert went to Europe with him. Inside, I had all kinds of unreasonable fears. For the first time, I was afraid for our relationship. *What if he leaves me? What if he really can't cope? What if it doesn't work out?* The trip to Europe lasted about three weeks. During that time I received letters and postcards from Switzerland, Germany, France, and other places they visited. The messages were all the same — that he missed me, loved me, and wished I was with him.

When he returned from Europe, he exploded into

the house. "I missed you so much, I couldn't wait to get back," he exclaimed. He did come back — more loving and sensitive than ever.

Donald and I began talking about the possibility of my being healed. Until now, I'd accepted my situation. But my desire to be a complete woman led me to fiercely claim promises I felt the Lord had put in His Word for me. *After all*, I reasoned, *He allows us to have experiences of suffering and sickness to teach us. I've learned an enormous amount through my accident. But now that I've learned what He had for me to learn, He might heal me!* This was to be a new adventure of faith — the next phase of spiritual development for me.

Of course, physiologically, I could not be healed — my injury was permanent. Yet I knew nothing was impossible for God. Did He not, through Christ, heal all kinds of paralysis and sicknesses? He even raised the dead.

Even today there are miracles of healing. I'd heard about many cases of "permanent," "incurable," or "fatal" diseases or injuries being reversed.

Donald and I read James 5 and other passages, concentrating on the idea that it was God's will for me to be healed. The Lord seemed to speak to us through John 14 and 15 and many other passages, and we prayed with renewed enthusiasm and thankfulness.

We believed that finding God's will was a matter of circumstances, faith in God's love, the assurance of His Word, and dependence on the power of His Holy Spirit. There was new optimism in the prospect of sharing our lives together.

"We're absolutely convinced that God wants me healed!" I told Diana.

"Joni, this whole thing is getting out of hand. You're twisting God's arm — blackmailing Him. You're not being realistic about this," she replied.

"Diana, I'm surprised that you'd say that. I thought you'd have more faith than that. You must have faith that God really does want to heal me," I said by way of rebuke.

Donald and I prayed that God would bring about the

circumstances for us to trust Him. I began to inform my friends that God was going to heal me soon. Each time Donald and I got together we prayed it would be soon.

"Lord, we have faith. We believe Your Word that You want us healthy and able to better serve You," prayed Donald.

"Thank You for the lessons in trust and patience that You have taught me through my suffering, Lord. And thank You for what You plan to do to bring glory to Yourself by healing me according to Your promises," I added.

As we continued to pray about this matter, we planned to attend a church service where the format of the healing ministry outlined in James 5 could be followed.

Several friends drove me to the church. Elders came and laid hands upon me and anointed me with oil, according to the scriptural injunction. They read promises from the Bible and prayed for me.

With all the faith, devotion, and spiritual commitment we could discover through our own inner resources, Donald and I prayed and trusted.

I wasn't anticipating immediate healing, but expected a slow recovery, since my rehabilitation alone had taken nearly two years. It was logical to think God would restore me gradually, I reasoned.

But after several attempts and many healing services, it became obvious that I wasn't going to be healed. I was able to accept the reality of the situation, but I was frustrated — probably more for Donald than myself. Donald was quiet, yet intense. He seemed to be questioning everything, reevaluating all that had happened. It was awkward, especially for him, after pinning so much to that prayer of faith which went "unanswered." His introspection was guarded, and he began spending more time away from me. I resented this, again jealous of his time.

When Steve came home on college break, he, Diana, and I discussed the possible reasons God did not answer our prayers.

"Why do you suppose He didn't want you healed?" Diana asked.

"I don't know."

Steve broke in, "You know, I was thinking about that when I read Hebrews 11 recently. You know the passage?"

"Yeah, it talks about the people of faith," I answered.

"Well, it also says there are two categories of people — those whose faith was rewarded and those whose faith was not. All kinds of miraculous, fantastic things happened to some. Others were 'sawn asunder,' 'saw not the promises,' or did not experience a visible reward."

"And you think I'm in the latter category?" I asked.

Steve leaned forward to make a point. "Uh-huh. I think so. For now, anyway. But not forever. Second Corinthians 5 tells about the wonderful resurrection body you'll have some day instead of a useless, earthly body. We're living in 'tabernacles' now — temporary dwellings. But someday we'll live in temples — heavenly bodies that are perfect and permanent."

"But what about those verses we read about faith?" I protested.

Steve grabbed my knee to emphasize his words — as if I could feel it. "But that's what I'm trying to say! Remember the faith healer who told you, 'I believe it is God's will that you be healed'?"

"Yes."

"Well, I believe it, too. I believe it's God's will for everyone to be healed. But maybe we just can't agree as to timetable. I believe it is His will, but apparently it doesn't have priority over other things. You will be healed, but probably not until you receive your glorified body."

"But God does heal other people," I argued.

"Yes, I know. I don't question His sovereignty on this," he replied.

Diana added, "But when He does heal someone supernaturally, He must have reasons for it. For instance, there seems to be a lot of examples of healing miracles overseas in cultures where missionaries work. When people don't have the written Word of God, maybe they need a more obvious witness — you know, like 'signs and wonders' — to attract them to Christ."

"Yeah, could be," I answered.

Steve went on to say, "In our culture, it wouldn't be appropriate or necessary. Some hot-shot, sensation-seeking press would change the focus and distort the whole situation. God wouldn't receive the glory, and the whole purpose would be lost."

"I think maybe that's the way it works," I remarked.

Diana nodded. "It's a dangerous misunderstanding of the Bible to say categorically that it's God's will that everyone be well. It's obvious everyone is not well."

"Right. We're trying for perfection, but we haven't attained it yet. We still sin. We still catch colds. We still break legs and necks," I said, adding, "The more I think about it, the more I'm convinced that God doesn't want everyone well. He uses our problems for His glory and our good." As I thought of this, I recalled several godly families touched by tragedy and disease. Many who truly love the Lord are often afflicted the most and fall into this category.

Man's dealing with God in our day and culture is based on His Word rather than "signs and wonders."

"You know," Steve said, "there's really no difference in God's power. Maybe you have greater credibility because of your chair than if you were out of it."

"What do you mean?"

"Remember the Greek word for the power of God? I think it's *dunamos*."

"Yeah, it's where we get the word *dynamite*."

"Or *dynamo*," Steve said. "They both mean great power. One is explosive energy. The other is controlled, useful energy. A healing experience would be like an explosive release of God's energy getting you out of the chair. But staying in the chair takes power, too — controlled energy flowing through you that makes it possible to cope."

Over the next few months, Donald and I talked about this and many other things; but one thing we now avoided was talking about our future.

Then one day when Donald came, I sensed an awkward quiet, a tenseness. Finally, in a low voice, he said, "Joni, I'm going to be counseling this summer up in New York at a *Young Life* camp. I'm leaving tomorrow. I just wanted to come and say good-by."

I thought, *That's good. Things have been a bit sour in our relationship lately. We both need a breather from each other – like the Europe trip.* But I was puzzled about the decisive inflection Donald gave to the word *good-by*.

"What do you mean, good-by? You'll be gone for several weeks, but — "

"No, Joni. This is it. I'm sorry. We never should have allowed this relationship to develop the way it has. I never should have kissed you. We never should have shared the things we shared. We never should have talked and dreamed of marriage. It was all a mistake."

"A mistake! What do you mean? You were the one who encouraged me! I was the one who didn't want to get involved. You've kissed me and held me. I went from fear to hope because you told me you loved me and wanted us to build a life together! Donald — I've shared things so deeply with you — more than I've shared with my own family. And you're just going to walk away, just like that? Now you're saying it's a mistake — that you were just leading me along?" My voice faltered as I desperately tried to put words and thoughts together.

Hot tears of rage and frustration made me want to throw myself on him and beat him with my fists. All I could do was sit there and sob.

"I wasn't leading you along, I swear it," Donald said firmly. "I sincerely thought I could do it. But I was wrong. It's impossible. It's all a mistake."

"Oh, dear God, what is this? Is it really happening?" Panic swept over me as I thought of Donald standing across the room saying good-by. *What happened?* He came into my life and made me feel so attractive and useful — a *woman*. I didn't think anyone would ever care for me as much as he had. I didn't think it possible I could love anyone as deeply as I loved him.

I tried to stop crying. "Maybe you need time to reconsider — "

"No, Joni. I've thought seriously about what I'm doing. There's no turning back. It's over. I'm sorry." With that, he turned and walked to the door.

"Donald! Don't leave me! Donald, wait!"

"Good-by, Joni," he said quietly and closed the door behind him.

"No! Oh, my God — why are You letting this happen? Why are You hurting me like this?"

Fourteen

And so, with a simple "good-by," Donald walked out of my life. My heart and mind raged. *How could he be so cruel after being so loving and tender?*

Yet, after I regained my composure, I saw that he hadn't meant to be cruel. It was simply his style — no jive, no hypocrisy, he had said.

I knew when he left that he was walking out for good. He gave me no false hopes, no wrong impressions. In the long run, it was the least painful of any method he could have used.

I learned that Dick and Donald, good friends since school days, had shared the problem with each other. Dick, who himself had had similar confusion in his relationship with me earlier, had warned Donald not to let his feelings for me get out of hand.

"I know exactly what Don is going through," Dick told me later. "I was confused and torn up inside after you wrote me from California that you wanted to be 'just friends.' I knew what you were doing, but I felt then — and still feel — very much in love with you. But I also

know you're right about what my being able to really face
up to all your injury means. I just don't know. But I was
willing to commit myself to making it work. Maybe you
knew me better; maybe you didn't believe I could handle
it. I don't know. In any event, since we've been 'just good
friends' the past two years, I was happy for you both when
you and Don fell in love. I prayed that he'd be able to do
whatever I couldn't and that you'd really be happy together."

"Then what went wrong?" I asked.

"I don't know. I began to see Don questioning the
relationship. Several times he confided to me that he
wished he'd never let his feelings for you get so out of
hand. I suppose he — being older and probably wiser
than me — saw what you saw with me: that many guys
really can't deal with the chair in the long run. Or, at
least it seems Don and I can't."

My hurt was even more painful as I continued to
hear about Donald second-hand. He wrote letters to kids
we had both been counseling. I was angry and resentful
when kids we both had prayed with and helped received
letters and were still close to Donald and I wasn't.

I'd been warned not to let my feelings for Donald get
out of hand. Jay and Diana had urged me many times to
be careful, but I didn't listen. Now my hopes and dreams
for marriage were hopelessly crushed.

Why, God? I don't understand why. My reactions
included rage at Donald, self-pity for myself, and jealous
anger at friends who were still close to him. A young high
school girl, a new Christian whom we had both coun-
seled, came over to read a letter she had received from
Donald telling how God was working in his life in exciting
ways. She, of course, didn't know what happened between us. She merely came over to share an encouraging,
newsy letter to her from Donald. My envy grew and hot
tears began to run down from the corners of my eyes.

When she left and I was by myself, I felt ashamed of
my attitudes. I wasn't handling this "irritation" with a
godly response. I turned to a familiar Scripture passage
for comfort — 1 Corinthians 13, the love chapter of the

Bible. But my mind played tricks with the words.

"Though I speak with the tongues of men and angels and have *lust*, I'm like sounding brass or crashing cymbals. If I have prophetic gifts, absolute faith, and lust, I amount to nothing. If I give away all that I have, even allow my body to be burned, and have lust, I achieve nothing. Lust is quick to lose patience; it is possessive; it tries to impress others and has inflated ideas of its own importance. Lust has bad manners and pursues selfish aims. It is touchy. . . ."

By substituting the word "lust" for "love," I saw what had gone wrong with our relationship. I had *lusted* after Donald — after his time, his attention, his presence — because I felt I had a right to. I saw what a consuming, fiery passion lust was. It was a desire that I did not want to deny myself. In the end, I lost everything that I sought to selfishly control.

Now the truth of 1 Corinthians 13 became evident. True love is unselfish, disciplined, directed, self-controlled, patient, and kind.

I began to sob bitterly at my confusion and hurt. This time, however, my hurt drove me to the Lord instead of to self-pity and self-centered introspection. I reread Scriptures which had helped me overcome previous disappointments.

I decided I didn't want to listen to the birds. They all reminded me of the beautiful times Donald and I had gone to the woods for quiet retreats and this was the only way I could consciously shut him out of my mind. It was difficult enough just to be outdoors with all those memories. How can I describe my feelings? For a year my mind had been working toward fulfillment of an ideal — my marriage to Donald; I had believed that our plans were part of God's perfect will for us. Then, in one brief day, my dream disintegrated before my eyes so completely that there was not a flicker of hope that it could be revived.

I recalled Steve's mention of Lamentations 3. He had once told me, "Joni, God must have His reasons. Jeremiah says that 'it is good that a young man bear the yoke in his youth.' Perhaps your life will have greater value in years to come because you're going through this experience now."

"Lord," I prayed, "what is happening to that 'excellent gift' I read about in Your Word? What are You doing?" I recalled passages from the Gospels in which Peter and John questioned Jesus as I was now doing. "What is that to thee?" was the Lord's simple, blunt reply. Jesus didn't coddle Peter or allow him to indulge in self-pity. The Lord said, in essence, "What do you care? It doesn't matter. You keep your eyes on me." I learned that God's truth is not always kind or comfortable. Sometimes His love for us involves harshness or a stern reproof.

I read other verses: "Welcome trials as friends," said the apostle James, reminding me of the lessons God had already taught me in the hospital and during the years that followed. "In everything give thanks. . . . All things work together. . . ."

I forced myself back into God's Word. There was no extensive self-pity, no wallowing in tears. God was merely providing me with yet another test — a "gut" testing of His truth, love, and purposes.

Letters from Donald to mutual friends were vibrant with his testimony of God at work in his life. He wrote of exciting spiritual growth and progress as the weeks turned into months. After the long summer, he wrote to friends telling of a lovely young woman he had met while working at the camp.

I felt the sting of hurt as I received the news that Donald had fallen in love with another woman. But the Lord seemed to say, "What is that to thee?"

I wrote to Steve, away at Bible college, and poured out my heart. He wrote back and assured me of his concern and prayers. His letter closed with a promise from Psalm 40: "His truth and lovingkindness shall continually preserve thee" — that whatever the hurt involved in this learning process, God always deals with us in love. This and other passages sustained me through this difficult period.

It was hard for me to accept the fact that Donald was not God's will, God's best for me. "But, Lord, if not Donald, I believe You have someone or something better for me. I will trust You to bring it into my life." I recalled hearing a preacher say *God never closes a door without opening a window — He always gives us something better when He takes something away.*

I took this promise at face value. It's obvious, looking back, that God did know best. I had read into circumstances, Scripture, and everything else all the right "meaning" to make Donald a part of my life. It was easy to say "God wants us happy, doesn't He?" and then bend verses to fit my purposes. I suppose I knew all along it wasn't going to work but pursued the idea that it was God's will that Donald build his life around me.

After my accident, I had clung to Dick, then Jay, Diana, and until now, Donald. I needed their love and support to satisfy my emotional needs. Now, however, I felt free. It was as if I had finally gained emotional independence through complete dependence on God. One day, while sitting outside in my wheelchair, I was quietly reflecting over these thoughts. *Lord*, I prayed, *I wish I could have seen this earlier — I wish I'd have remembered that Your grace is sufficient for me.* As I sat there on the quiet wooded lawn, verse after verse came to mind to comfort me. *Please, Lord, make Yourself real to me just now.*

Peace of mind and inner joy flooded my mind and soul. Then I looked up. Almost as a symbol of God's love and reassurance, a butterfly from high among the trees fluttered within inches of me. It was both startling and beautiful.

"Lord, thank You for Your goodness. Sending that butterfly at precisely this instant was a creative, subtle way of testifying to Your quiet and understated presence." I promised myself to think of God's goodness every time I saw a butterfly.

I reflected over this most unusual and difficult summer during long outdoor retreats with the Lord. I sought to be outside and meditate on His purposes, so to occupy myself during these times, I devoted all my time and energy to my art; I found a renewed interest in drawing. And it seemed my art was getting better. There was a quality that hadn't been there before. I didn't know what it was, but others noticed the difference too.

It was a slow transition, but not as difficult as I had expected. I saw Donald in a new light, with greater understanding. He had done what was right and best, even if it hurt us both, for I know now that it hurt him as much as it hurt me.

We were both blind to the serious consequences of what such a relationship would mean. When we're in love, our love takes expression in actions. If there is nowhere to go, in reality, then wishful thinking and fantasy convince us that "everything will work out." People warn us, but we choose not to believe them.

Many young people ignore reality. They know something is wrong, that a relationship won't work, but they go ahead anyway, as we would have done, convinced by wishful thinking.

I look back now and thank God for our relationship. There are so many things I never would have learned if Donald had not come into my life and left me, and so I thank the Lord for this experience. I'm especially grateful God helped me deal with our separation without lingering feelings of bitterness or despair.

I even accepted Donald's new love with honest joy that he, too, had at last found God's perfect will for his life. At a Bible study one evening, a friend came up to me. Hesitantly, he said, "Uh — Joni, I want to tell you something before you hear it from someone else."

"Jimmy, you don't have to say anything more. I know."

"You do? You've already heard that Donald is engaged? How?"

"I don't know," I smiled. "I guess I just knew it, that's all."

I was shocked at how easily God helped me meet what should have been a hurtful, difficult meeting. And when Donald brought Sandy, a beautiful, young widow who had lost her husband in an accident, to Bible study three weeks later, we were seated next to one another.

She knew about me. In any other situation, this would have been awkward, to say the least. But I turned to her, a tall, lovely woman whose dark features complemented Donald's own good looks, and said, "Sandy, I'm really glad to meet you. I want you to know how genuinely happy I am for you and Donald."

She smiled and said thank you.

I told her, "I pray for you both every night. I praise God for what He's done in all three of our lives. I'm really excited about you both — especially your willingness to serve Christ." And I meant every word.

Friends and family members who knew how deeply Donald and I had cared for one another were amazed at my attitude. They had expected me to fall apart. And I probably would have gone to pieces if I had not allowed God to handle the situation.

I really began to see suffering in a new light — not as trials to avoid, but as opportunities to "grab," because God gives so much of His love, grace, and goodness to those who do.

My life changed more during the last half of 1972 than any other period of my life — even my previous five years in the chair.

When Donald walked out of my life, there was no one in whom I could put my trust — except God. And since the Lord had always proved Himself faithful before, I trusted Him now.

Fifteen

During the fall of 1972, I began to ask serious questions about my future. "Lord," I asked, "if not college, if not Donald, then what? What do You have for me?"

I believed that if God took something away from me, He would always replace it with something better. My experience had taught me this as I relied on the sovereignty of God. "Delight thyself in God," the psalmist said, "trust in His way." As I did so, it became easier to express true gratitude for what He brought into my life — good as well as suffering.

The suffering and pain of the past few years had been the ingredients that had helped me mature emotionally, mentally, and spiritually. I felt confident and independent, trusting in the Lord for my physical and emotional needs.

Pain and suffering have purpose. We don't always see this clearly. The apostle Paul suffered for Christ. His experience included imprisonment, beatings, stonings, shipwreck and some physical "thorn in the flesh." The blessing of suffering is, as J. B. Phillips interprets Romans 5:3-5, " . . . we can be full of joy here and now even in our trials and troubles. Taken in the right spirit, these very things will give us patient endurance; this in turn will develop a mature character, and a character of this sort produces a steady hope, a hope that will never disappoint us."

I believed He was working in my life to create grace and wisdom out of the chaos of pain and depression.

Now all these experiences began to find visible expression in my art. At first, I drew for fun; then, to occupy my time; finally, to express my feelings for what God was doing in me. I sensed, somehow, that my artwork fit into the scheme of things. Perhaps it would be the "something better."

But the last thing I wanted was for people to admire my drawings simply because they were drawn by someone in a wheelchair holding a pen in her mouth. I wanted my work to be good in itself — in creativity and craftsmanship. That's why I was both pleased and proud at having my work displayed in a local art festival — for its own sake, and not because of my handicap.

For the first time, I threw myself fully into my artwork. I sketched pictures of things that had beauty rather than things that expressed emotions or hurts I'd experienced. It was a positive collection, with hope reflected in the drawings of animals, scenes, and people. As a result, people accepted them. They were attracted to sketches of youngsters, mountains, flowers, and forest animals because of the common beauty such subjects expressed.

I honestly felt God had brought me to this place and had even greater blessings in store. I never would have believed this a year or two earlier, but I had now come to the place where the "something better" was in being single. I read in 1 Corinthians 6 and 7 that there could be a calling higher than marriage for some. A single woman could devote herself to being holy with fewer distractions if she had no husband, family, or house to care for, and I was free from a house-oriented routine. True, I did not have the pleasures and privileges that went with such a role, but God had substituted other joys, and I was more than fulfilled. I had my own freedom to come and go without having to maintain a schedule involving others. I could travel, keep late work hours, read, talk, or whatever I choose. It was a great freedom.

People often said to me, "You had no choice about being single. That's why you can accept that role more easily than I can. That's why you can be joyful. But I am lonely, frustrated, and unfulfilled."

"I'm not sure it's easier for me," I told them. "Every person who is faced with the prospect of singlehood should trust God's wisdom. Because I did not trust Him for my own life but sought to engineer His will in my relationship with Donald, I was also frustrated. But when I had no choice but acceptance, trust, and surrender, this did become easy for me. If we accept this handicap from God, we are freed from the constant agony and anxiety of wondering, worrying, and desperate searching. Not knowing the future and worrying about it causes most of our bitterness and grief."

"You mean I should give up hoping to be married at all?" a girl asked me once.

"I'm saying that acceptance of the role of being single ends the frustration of not knowing," I replied. "But that's the hardest part. Surrender to the idea of being forever single, with all the sacrifices that implies, is the most difficult. But once acceptance is made, living with that role is easier."

"That sounds like just giving up," she observed.

"Maybe it is. This is not to say God will never allow us to marry someday. Maybe He will; maybe He won't. What I'm saying is that it doesn't matter because we leave the choice and decision with Him. We trust His judgment that 'all things work together for our good' if we love God."

"But I feel I have needs to be fulfilled — that I have a right to be married!"

"Only God is capable of telling us what our rights and needs are. You have to surrender that right to Him.

Begin your life as a single person, working and living according to the priorities of serving and glorifying Him. In turn, God gives a rich and satisfying life. In place of one partner, He brings many friends into our lives to meet our emotional needs and loneliness."

"That's what you've experienced, Joni?"

"Yes. And it gets better. Maybe, God will give you back that right to be married after you surrender it completely. He may bring someone into your life after all. But holding tightly onto that hope and thinking constantly about the possibility of it happening is terribly frustrating."

Young people listened respectfully when I shared these concepts with them. But I could always see the reservation and holding back in their eyes. It was difficult for them to comprehend how a handicap of being single could be better than the joys of marriage.

"Scripture says," I reminded them, "in 1 Corinthians, 'Eye hath not seen, nor ear heard, neither have entered into the heart of men, the things which God hath prepared for them that love him.' The apostle was comparing the natural man with the spiritual man in this passage, but I also think it could apply to us concerning our future."

"What do you mean?" a girl asked me one day.

"Well, we think of the greatest experiences of love, tenderness, and feelings we might have with a guy — all the beautiful things that have entered into the heart, mind, eye and ear. God is saying *These are nothing compared to what lies ahead*. I still don't know what this means. But I've found that God never places any real emphasis on the present — except as preparation for the future. We only have a limited sense of reality. This doesn't mean I'm preoccupied with heaven and the hereafter. It just helps me put things into perspective."

"But don't you think that's true for you because you're in a wheelchair?" someone usually asked.

"No, I don't think so. This is a universal truth. A lot of people who aren't in wheelchairs still have to deal with being single, just as I do. It can be a source of constant irritation and frustration, or it can be a joy."

"You mean you believe you'll never marry?"

"No. I have no feeling one way or the other. I'm not sure that I will never marry. Or that I will. I'm content, whether I marry or not."

"Well, what about those of us who haven't come to that place where we can accept that role as easily as you?"

"If you're single, with no plans or prospects, just live as though God will have you remain single until He brings someone or something better into your life."

"Sort of like that verse you quoted — 'eye hath not seen, nor ear heard,' right?" someone asked.

"Yes. Sometimes I recall experiences of feeling — of running through grassy fields, swimming in a cool, clear stream, climbing up a rugged mountain, smelling flowers, riding a horse — all the sensations I'd have on my feet. But God says all of this together can't compare with the glory and future reality He has prepared for me. It's as I said before — the future is the only reality that counts. The only thing we can take to heaven with us is our character. Our character is all we have to determine what kind of a being we will be for all eternity. It's what we *are* that will be tested by fire. Only the qualities of Christ in our character will remain."

I was grateful for these opportunities to explain how God was working in my life. I began to see a mature purpose in all His dealings with me, and I was happier than I had ever been. My experiences charged me with creative energy and a maturity I didn't have before, and my art had a new quality and professionalism.

I experimented with various papers, pens, pencils, and charcoal. I tried different approaches and techniques, finally settling on the elements that seemed to work best. Using a sharp, felt-tip *Flair* pen, I sketched with precision and control. I gave drawings to friends as wedding presents and Christmas gifts. This demand for my art kept me fairly busy. However, I had still not found an outlet for my drawings which would enable me to derive income from them and become gainfully employed — and more independent.

Then one day an insurance executive called on my father at his downtown office. Neill Miller is an energetic, good-natured, successful, Christian businessman. He is Senior Field Underwriter for the Aetna Life and Casualty Company, as well as being actively involved with several Baltimore charity drives. Neill Miller sees opportunities where other people see obstacles. Through his efforts, national celebrities have become interested in the causes he represents and have volunteered their services and talents.

During his visit with dad, Mr. Miller noticed one of my drawings on the wall of the office.

"I really like that drawing, Mr. Eareckson. Is it an original?" he asked.

"Yes. As a matter of fact, my daughter drew it," dad replied.

"Really? She's quite an artist. It has a great deal of character as well as realistic detail. She has an original style — it shows unusual discipline," observed Mr. Miller.

"Thank you. I'll tell her." Then dad said, "You might be interested to know Joni — that's my daughter — is paralyzed. She has to draw holding the pen in her mouth."

"That's even more remarkable!" Mr. Miller stood up and examined the drawing more closely. "Amazing. Absolutely amazing."

"She's never had any formal training," dad explained. "I've dabbled in art most of my life, and I suppose she's inherited my interest in art. But her talent and style are her own."

"Has she exhibited her art?" Mr. Miller asked.

"No, not really — just at a couple festivals. She does it for fun. She draws for friends and family mostly."

"Well, we can't let such talent go unnoticed," exclaimed Mr. Miller. "Do you think she'd object if I arranged a small art exhibit for her?"

"Why, I'm sure she'd be delighted."

"Fine! Let me see what I can do. I'll be in touch."

Mr. Miller telephoned dad later to say that he had arranged for a small exhibition at a local restaurant. Dad took all the original drawings I'd been working on for the past several months to the Town and Country Restaurant in the center of downtown Baltimore. The Town and Country is a popular, prestigious gathering place for local businessmen and important political figures.

I expected a small, informal gathering of people to look at my drawings, chat, and go on their way, as that was the pattern I'd observed at several other art exhibits with other artists. I secretly hoped I might even be able to sell one or two drawings.

Jay, Diana, and I drove downtown the morning of the exhibit. We had been told to arrive at ten o'clock. As Jay turned onto South Street toward the restaurant, we found the avenue blocked off.

"That's strange," I remarked. They're not working on the road or anything. Why would they block off a main street like this?"

"I don't know. I'll turn down this side street and cut over," said Jay.

"Wait. You can't get through there either. There's a policeman directing traffic."

"It must be something for the Chamber of Commerce," remarked Diana.

"Yeah. Maybe a Lincoln's birthday parade or something," added Jay.

"It must be a parade — look," I exclaimed.

"A big brass band. How exciting. Too bad we're going to the exhibit. We could watch it," Jay smiled.

"Maybe you can turn down — " I didn't finish the sentence.

We all saw it at the same time and gasped, unbelieving.

The brass band was in front of the Town and Country. And blazoned across the front of the building was a huge banner declaring "Joni Eareckson Day." A television camera crew was standing there waiting, along with a growing crowd of people.

"Oh, no! What's happening?" I cried. "Jay, quick! Turn into the alley before they see us!"

The car came to a stop between the buildings, comfortably out of sight of the commotion.

"What am I going to do?" I asked Jay. "This is incredible. What has he done?"

"Oh, wow, Joni. I've never seen anything like this. He did say 'small' exhibition, didn't he?"

We sat there several minutes trying to decide what to do. When it was obvious we had no choice but to go ahead with the event, Jay backed the car around and pulled up to the restaurant.

I prayed inwardly that Jay, in her own nervousness, would not drop me as she and Mr. Miller lifted me from the car into my wheelchair.

I said under my breath, "Mr. Miller, what have you done?" But before he could explain, I was besieged.

Reporters from the Baltimore *News-American* and local NBC television affiliate were asking questions. I blinked and sheepishly tried to collect my thoughts. A liveried, chauffeur-driven representative of FTD brought me a beautiful bouquet of roses. An official from city hall was reading a proclamation from the mayor announcing a local art appreciation week and honoring me in "Joni Eareckson Day" ceremonies. I was overwhelmed and somewhat embarrassed at all the attention.

I said to Mr. Miller, "Is all this really necessary?" I thought perhaps the entire focus of the exhibit would be lost or at least misconstrued, with everyone's attention turning to the wheelchair. Yet, as the event unfolded, that was not the case at all, and I apologized for my hasty judgment. Perhaps I'd grown too sensitive in this area, half-expecting the usual pity and put-down accorded to people in wheelchairs. I had already experienced (a fact confirmed by the National Paraplegic Foundation) the difficulty of getting people who didn't know me to accept me as an intellectual equal.

Perhaps I overreact to this type of situation, but I am intensely interested in getting people to relate to me, my art, or my Christian witness strictly on their own merits. I don't want my chair to be the overriding focus as I talk to people, whether about art or Christ.

I'm not upset about the chair, so don't you be, I want to tell people.

The ceremonies were excellent, and the focus on my art was not lost. The questions of reporters dealt primarily with my art; the chair was merely background.

Mr. Miller told me, "Joni, your sights are set too low. You don't realize just how good your art is. I'm sorry if all this embarrassed you at first. But I guess I don't believe in doing things in a small way."

The excitement peaked following the ceremonies, and the rest of the exhibit followed the standard procedures for such events.

People asked:

"Where do you get the ideas for your drawings?"

"How long does it take to complete a picture?"

"Did you study art professionally?"

When the crowd thinned at one point, Mr. Miller brought a tall, good-looking young man over and introduced him. His hands were stuffed into the pockets of his jacket, and he looked uncomfortable.

"I wanted him to talk to you, Joni," Mr. Miller said and walked away, leaving us awkwardly looking at one another.

"I'm happy to meet you," I said. "Won't you sit down?" He sat at the nearby table without speaking, and I began to feel uneasy.

Why was he here? He didn't seem to want to talk to me. My efforts at small talk were hopeless. Yet I could tell by his eyes something was bothering him.

Trying once more, I asked, "What do you do?"

"Nothing." Then, almost as a concession, he muttered, "I used to be a fireman. But I can't work now."

"Oh?" *What do I say now?* "Uh — will you tell me about it?"

"It was an accident."

"Yes?"

He shuffled nervously in his seat. "Look," he said, "I don't know why I'm here. Miller told me I ought to come and talk to you — that you had a rough time a while back with — uh — with your handicap."

"Yeah — I sure did. I guess I'd have killed myself if I'd been able to use my arms. I was really depressed. But — " I paused, letting him know I still didn't know what his problem was.

His handsome young face was contorted with anguish. He raised his arms, taking his hands from his coat pockets. But he had no hands — only scarred stumps where they had been amputated.

"Look at these ugly stumps!" he said. "My hands were burned in a fire — and they're *gone*. And I just can't cope!"

The frustration, pent-up rage, and bitterness poured out as his voice broke.

"I'm sorry," I told him, "but Mr. Miller was right. I can help you, I think."

"How?" he said sharply. "I'll never get my hands back."

"I know. I don't mean to sound glib. But I've been where you are. I know the anger, the feelings of unfairness — of being robbed, cheated of your self-respect. I had those same feelings. Maybe it's worse for a man — you know, trying to be independent and self-supporting. But I think I can identify with you."

I told him something of my own experiences at the hospital and Greenoaks. I told him that his feelings were natural.

"But how'd you get over it? How do you cope with your handicap? You're cheerful, not at all cynical today. Where do you get the power to pull it off?" he asked.

"Boy, that's quite a story. Would you like to hear it?"

He nodded. I told him how a relationship with Jesus Christ gives access to God and all His power. I shared how God had been working in my life the past few years and how He alone helped me face my fears and take on the tasks of living. Then I shared with him the simple gospel message I had heard as a fifteen-year-old at *Young Life* camp.

His face brightened as we talked. For nearly a half hour, I shared the principles God had taught me. When he left, he said, "Thanks, Joni. Neill Miller was right. You have helped me. I'll try again. Thanks."

(Today, this young man is enthusiastic about life again and is chief spokesman in the school system for the city fire department.)

Meanwhile, the exhibit at the Town and Country drew to a close, and Neill Miller's idea turned out to be the event that launched my art career. By early evening, I was stunned to learn I'd sold about a thousand dollars' worth of original drawings at fifty to seventy-five dollars each!

The event also got exposure for my work on Channel 11 in Baltimore: in addition to covering the exhibit, they invited me to be on a local talk show and feature my art.

Seymour Kopf, of the Baltimore *News-American*, carried a full feature in his column.

"Why do you sign your drawings 'PTL'?" Mr. Kopf had asked. He recorded my full answer in his column:

"It stands for 'praise the Lord.' You see, Mr. Kopf, God loves us — He *does care*. For those who love God, everything — even what happened to me at age seventeen — works together for good. God has been good to me. He has ingrained the reflection of Christ into my character, developed my happiness, my patience, my purpose in life. He has given me contentment. My art is a reflection of how God can empower someone like me to rise above circumstances."

I was invited to participate in local art shows later that spring. The exhibit also opened the doors for me to address Christian women's clubs, schools, church groups, and civic functions where I not only showed my art, but shared my Christian testimony as well. I even made a special tour of the White House, where I left one of my drawings for First Lady, Pat Nixon.

Other TV and radio appearances were offered, and each new contact seemed to generate additional stories or appearances.

On the strength of growing art sales, I was thrilled to

see a small measure of independence. I wouldn't have to be a financial burden on anyone but would now be able to earn my own money. I even created a line of greeting cards and prints from several of my drawings, and these began to sell well, too. We named this company *Joni PTL*, and it expanded rapidly.

About this time, a close friend, Andy Byrd, told me of his plan to buy a Christian bookstore franchise and open a store; he wondered if I would like to have a partnership. We talked to Ken Wagner who became a third partner.

Our plans were not only exciting but seemed like a solid business investment. A Christian bookstore was something many of us had prayed for as a necessary element for Western Baltimore.

Finally, in September, 1973, after months of plans, prayer, and hard work, there was a grand opening of the Logos Bookstore, 1120 North Rolling Road, in the Rolling Road Plaza shopping mall. Just before the store opened, amid boxes of materials, books to price, and supplies, we prayed. Our prayer of dedication was for the many secular-oriented shoppers passing by — that our store would be a center of Christian concern and outreach where people could come for help.

I used the store as a center for selling original art and prints of several originals. These sold almost as quickly as I drew them. Between the bookstore, speaking engagements, and art fairs or festivals, it was difficult to keep up with the demand.

I developed a brief testimony sheet which I printed and handed out at art shows while I was drawing. It explained my unusual drawing methods and faith in Christ and became a great tool for counseling and witnessing as people who came to watch stopped to chat and discuss the power of God in my life.

Through all the activities and events, there was one overriding focus to all this: that, humanly speaking, my art would help me gain independence, and, more importantly, that it would be used to glorify God.

Sixteen

I was sitting outside at the ranch at Sykesville one beautiful late summer morning in 1974 when a telephone call came for me.

"Miss Eareckson, I'm calling from the 'Today Show' in New York. We'd like you to come on the program and tell your story and show your drawings. Can you come?"

My heart was in my throat. The "Today Show"!

"Of course," I replied. "I'll be glad to come." Jay stood by the phone writing down the information. We agreed on an appearance for September 11.

Jay drove me to New York, taking our friends Sherri Pendergrass and Cindy Blubaugh to help. After getting settled at the hotel the day before the scheduled appearance, we went over to Rockefeller Center to meet with the director. He explained the procedure to me, and we discussed possible interview questions. He made me feel relaxed and comfortable, not only with the mental preparation for the show, but with the line of questioning the hostess, Barbara Walters, was likely to take.

Early the next morning I found myself sitting opposite Barbara Walters. Lights flooded the set with warmth
and brightness. Miss Walters smiled and glanced
quickly at her notes.

"Just relax, Joni," she said warmly. "Are you comfortable?"

"Yes. Thank you."

"Fine."

"Fifteen seconds!" someone called from behind the
cameras.

I wasn't as nervous as I thought I might be —
probably because I was secure in what I was planning to
say and knowing that my testimony would be shared with
so many millions of people. I didn't know what Miss
Walters planned to ask me, but I knew of nothing she
could ask that would make me uncomfortable.

"Ten seconds."

Lord, I prayed quickly, *give me confidence, wisdom,
opportunity. Make this all meaningful.*

"Five." I swallowed and wet my lips, watching the
floor director count down with his fingers. "Three, two,
one."

A red light on top of one of the cameras went on, and
Barbara Walters turned toward it.

"We want to show you a collection of drawings
which we have in the studio today," she said. "And, as
you'll see, they're drawings that have been obviously
executed with artistic skill and what would seem to be a
fine hand. But they were drawn in a manner unlike, I
believe, any pictures you've ever seen before. The artist
is Joni Eareckson of Baltimore, Maryland."

Then she turned to me, and the interview began. I
don't recall all I said, except that Miss Walters made it
natural and enjoyable. Her questions were interesting
and not at all threatening. I liked her instantly and had
the feeling I knew her, that she was an old friend.

The camera also took in a display of my drawings as
we talked. The interview lasted ten minutes before Miss
Walters broke for station identification. Then while the
affiliate stations around the country cut away for local

news, she interviewed me for another five minutes for New York City viewers.

I was able to say everything I wanted to say. Miss Walters thanked me and resumed her duties with other features of the show for that day.

Eleanor McGovern, wife of the senator, was also a guest that morning. She and I talked at length after the show went off the air. She told me how her husband, George, the former Democratic presidential candidate, had discovered some of the same values and concepts that I had learned. "It was when he studied for the ministry, before he became interested in politics," Mrs. McGovern explained, and we chatted about her own spiritual values and beliefs. I gave her a drawing of Christ I'd done, and we exchanged addresses to keep in touch with one another.

As the production crew began putting things away, turning off lights and putting lens caps on the cameras, I finally had time to reflect on what had happened.

"Just think," remarked Jay, "you probably talked to twenty or thirty million people this morning about your faith. That's quite an opportunity!"

Mr. Al Nagle, president, and Mr. John Preston, vice president, of the PaperMate Division of the Gillette Company were each watching that morning. Having noticed I was using a *Flair* pen, their company arranged several national exhibits.

Many other people watching the "Today Show" that morning wrote to me. Some wanted prints of my art work, others ordered greeting cards, and still others asked questions about my experiences.

My first exhibit sponsored by PaperMate was held in Chicago at the prestigious Rubino Galleries on LaSalle Street in the shadow of the famous John Hancock Center.

I exhibited my art and demonstrated my drawing for a week. During that time, I was interviewed by the *Chicago Tribune* and *Sun-Times*. I also appeared on the CBS-TV affiliate in Chicago, "The Lee Phillip Show."

When we returned home, again a flood of mail greeted me. I began to be swamped with requests for additional interviews. Art exhibits were scheduled for Lincoln Center in New York and Atlantic Richfield Plaza in Los Angeles. Scores of churches and Christian groups contacted me to come and speak. *Women's Day, People, Teen,* and *Coronet* magazines asked for interviews. *Campus Life* did a four-page story. *Moody Monthly* and *Christian Life* also did stories. There were more radio and TV appearances.

I could see how the Lord was going to use the "Today Show" to broaden my scope of witness and open many new doors.

Epilogue

"Wouldn't it be exciting if right now, in front of you, I could be miraculously healed, get up out of my chair and on my feet? What a miracle! We'd all be excited and praising God. It'd be something we could confirm for ourselves. We'd actually see the wonder and power of God. Wouldn't that be thrilling?" I was speaking to an audience of 1,600 young people.

I paused as they visualized that scene. Then I continued, "But far more exciting and wonderful in the long run would be the miracle of your salvation — the healing of your own soul. You see, that's more exciting because that's something that will last forever. If my body were suddenly and miraculously healed, I'd be on my feet another thirty or forty years; then my body dies. But a soul lives for eternity. From the standpoint of eternity, my body is only a flicker in the time-span of forever."

Afterwards, someone asked me, "Do you suppose you were so strong-willed and stubborn that the only way God could work in your life was to 'zap' you and put you in a wheelchair?"

I shook my head. "In the Psalms we're told that God does not deal with us according to our sins and iniquities. My accident was not a punishment for my wrongdoing — whether or not I deserved it. Only God knows *why* I was paralyzed. Maybe He knew I'd be ultimately happier serving Him. If I were still on my feet, it's hard to say how things might have gone. I probably would have drifted through life — marriage, maybe even divorce — dissatisfied and disillusioned. When I was in high school, I reacted to life selfishly and never built on any long-lasting values. I lived simply for each day and the pleasure I wanted — and almost always at the expense of others."

"But now you're happy?" a teen-age girl asked.

"I really am. I wouldn't change my life for anything. I even feel privileged. God doesn't give such special attention to everyone and intervene that way in their lives. He allows most people to go right on in their own ways. He doesn't interfere even though He knows they are ultimately destroying their lives, health, or happiness, and it must grieve Him terribly. I'm really thankful He did something to get my attention and change me. You know, you don't have to get a broken neck to be drawn to God. But the truth is, people don't always listen to the experiences of others and learn from them. I hope you'll learn from my experience, though, and not have to go through the bitter lessons of suffering which I had to face in order to learn."

In the months after the Chicago trip, I began to see the chair as a tool to create an unusual classroom situation. It was particularly gratifying to see many young people commit themselves to Christ after my sharing with them. This, too, was "something better."

I understood why Paul could "rejoice in suffering," why James could "welcome trials as friends," and why Peter did "not think it strange in the testing of your faith." All of these pressures and difficulties had ultimate positive ends and resulted in "praise, honor, and glory" to Christ.

I quietly thanked God for the progress He had

helped me make. I recalled how at the hospital a few years earlier someone had told me, "Just think of all the crowns you'll receive in heaven for your suffering."

"I don't want any crowns," I had barked back. "I want to be back on my feet."

Now my thought was, "Good grief, if I'm winning crowns, I can't wait to get more because it's the one thing I can give to the Lord Jesus Christ when I meet Him."

I am actually excited at these opportunities "to suffer for His sake" if it means I can increase my capacity to praise God in the process. Maybe it sounds glib or irresponsible to say that. Yet, I really do feel my paralysis is unimportant.

Circumstances have been placed in my life for the purpose of cultivating my character and conforming me to reflect Christlike qualities. And there is another purpose. Second Corinthians 1:37 explains it in terms of our being able to comfort others facing the same kinds of trials.

Wisdom is *trusting* God, not asking "Why, God?" Relaxed and in God's will, I know He is in control. It is not a blind, stubborn, stoic acceptance, but getting to know God and realize He is worthy of my trust. Although I am fickle and play games, God does not; although I have been up and down, bitter and doubting, He is constant, ever-loving.

James, the apostle, wrote to people who were being torn apart by lions. Certainly their lot was far worse than mine. If this Word was sufficient for their needs, it can definitely meet mine.

At this writing, the year 1975 is just ending. I am sitting in my chair backstage at a large auditorium in Kansas City. I've been asked to speak to nearly 2,000 kids in a Youth for Christ rally tonight.

I have had several moments to pause and reflect behind the heavy curtains that separate me from the audience. My mind has roamed back through the scenes of the past eight years. Familiar faces of family and friends come to mind. Jay, Diana, Dick, Donald, my parents, Steve — people God has brought into my life to

help bend and mold me more closely to Christ's image.
I can, and *do*, praise Him for it all — laughter and
tears, fun and pain. All of it has been a part of "growing in grace." The girl who became emotionally dis-
traught and wavered at each new set of circumstances is
now grown up, a woman who has learned to rely on God's
sovereignty.

I hear the voice of YFC director Al Metzger intro-
ducing me. Suddenly the purpose of my being here is
once again brought sharply into focus. In the next thirty
minutes, I will speak to 2,000 kids, telling them how God
transformed an immature and headstrong teen-ager into a
self-reliant young woman who is learning to rejoice in
suffering. I will have a unique opportunity. What I share
with them may determine where they will spend eternity,
so I approach this responsibility seriously.

I will talk to them about the steps God took in my life
— and explain His purposes, as I understand them, to
the present. In the process, I will share the concepts of
God's loving nature, His character, the purposes of
Christ's coming, and the reality of sin and repentance.

Al Metzger, the YFC director, is finishing his introduction now. Chuck Garriott carries my easel on stage
while his wife, Debbie, wheels my chair into the glare of
the footlights. As the applause dies down, I quiet my
thoughts and pray for the Holy Spirit to once again use my
words and experience to speak to people. Hopefully,
here — as in other meetings — scores of kids will
respond to God. But I will be pleased if only one person is
drawn to Christ.

Even one person would make the wheelchair worth
all that the past eight years have cost.